VIVARAIS REVISITED

Featuring the metre gauge systems in the Ardèche and Haute-Loire

John Organ

Front cover: SLM Mallet no.403 was viewed at Le Cheylard, having arrived with a special steam hauled charter from Dunières organised by FACS, on 10th May 1963. Note the large transhipment shed alongside the train. (Colour-Rail)

Rear cover upper: CFV publicity officer, Fabien Mottet, was observed checking the injectors of SACM Mallet no.414, prior to the locomotive hauling a service train to Lamastre on 12th September 2006. (J.F.Organ)

Rear cover lower: Built in the 15th century, the "Grand Pont" at Douce Plage is located at the lower entrance to the Doux Gorge. (P.Barnes)

Published July 2007

ISBN 978 1 906008 08 6

© Middleton Press, 2007

Design Deborah Esher

Published by
    Middleton Press
    Easebourne Lane
    Midhurst
    West Sussex
    GU29 9AZ
Tel: 01730 813169
Fax: 01730 812601
Email: info@middletonpress.co.uk
www.middletonpress.co.uk

Printed & bound by Biddles Ltd, Kings Lynn

CONTENTS

1. RÉSEAU DU VIVARAIS 1890 – 1968
2. VIVARAIS AND LOZÈRE LOCOMOTIVES AND RAILCARS
3. ROLLING STOCK OF THE CFD VIVARAIS AND LOZÈRE
4. LE CHEMIN DE FER DU VIVARAIS
5. VOIES FERRÉES DU VELAY
6. THE 60cm GAUGE CONNECTION
7. CFV AND VFV LOCOMOTIVES, RAILCARS AND CARRIAGES

ACKNOWLEDGEMENTS

The production of this publication has only been possible with the invaluable assistance of many individuals, in both France and Britain. My grateful thanks are therefore accorded to Messrs. J.Arrivetz, P.Barnes, F.Collardeau (SGVA), M.Knight, J.C.Laboureau, R.Lemon, J.Marsh, F.Mottet (CFV), J-L.Rochaix, D.Trevor Rowe, D.Smith, H.Tenoux (VFV), R.White (Colour-Rail) and J.A.Wood. Although all have contributed towards the completion of the project, I must particularly thank Fabien Mottet, Publicity and Marketing Officer of the CFV. Fabien's enthusiasm and encouragement throughout the compilation of the publication has resulted in far more material being made available than I could possibly have hoped for. In addition to his official capacity with the CFV, Fabien is also one of the locomotive staff, with the result that I was privileged to join him on the footplate of Mallet no.414 in September 2006. My sincere thanks are due to him for providing me with an unforgettable experience. Finally, I must thank my wife Brenda, who has once again tolerated my deep involvement in the project during the period of research and compilation.

INTRODUCTION

In 1999, Middleton Press published my first book *Vivarais Narrow Gauge*, which was produced to coincide with the 30th Anniversary of the re-opening of the Tournon to Lamastre section of the Vivarais system in June 1969. As this original book has recently become out of print, it is now an opportune time to publish an updated full colour edition. With so many developments having taken place at Tournon since 1999, the most notable being the formation of a new company to operate Le Chemin de Fer du Vivarais (CFV), the story of this fascinating railway can be brought up to date. Additionally, the Voies Ferrées du Velay (VFV) based at Dunières has continued to develop its operation during the last decade. There is now a growing relationship between the CFV and VFV, which can only be for the future benefit of both concerns.

Viewed from left to right, Jean Arrivetz, Brenda Organ and the author were discussing Vivarais history inside the elegant interior of the De Dietrich Inspection Saloon during September 1998. (F. Collardeau)

As this publication contains wholly colour illustrations, the majority are of necessity from the preservation era. Colour views of both the Vivarais and Lozère in their hey-day are unfortunately not as plentiful as the monochrome photographs taken prior to 1968. As a consequence there are sadly some locations, locomotives and carriages, that are not included in this volume, simply due to the lack of availability. However, these omissions were amply covered in my previous books covering the CFD operations in the Ardèche and Haute-Loire, *Vivarais Narrow Gauge* and *Southern France Narrow Gauge*. The latter is still available, published by Middleton Press.

Part 1 - RÉSEAU DU VIVARAIS 1890-1968

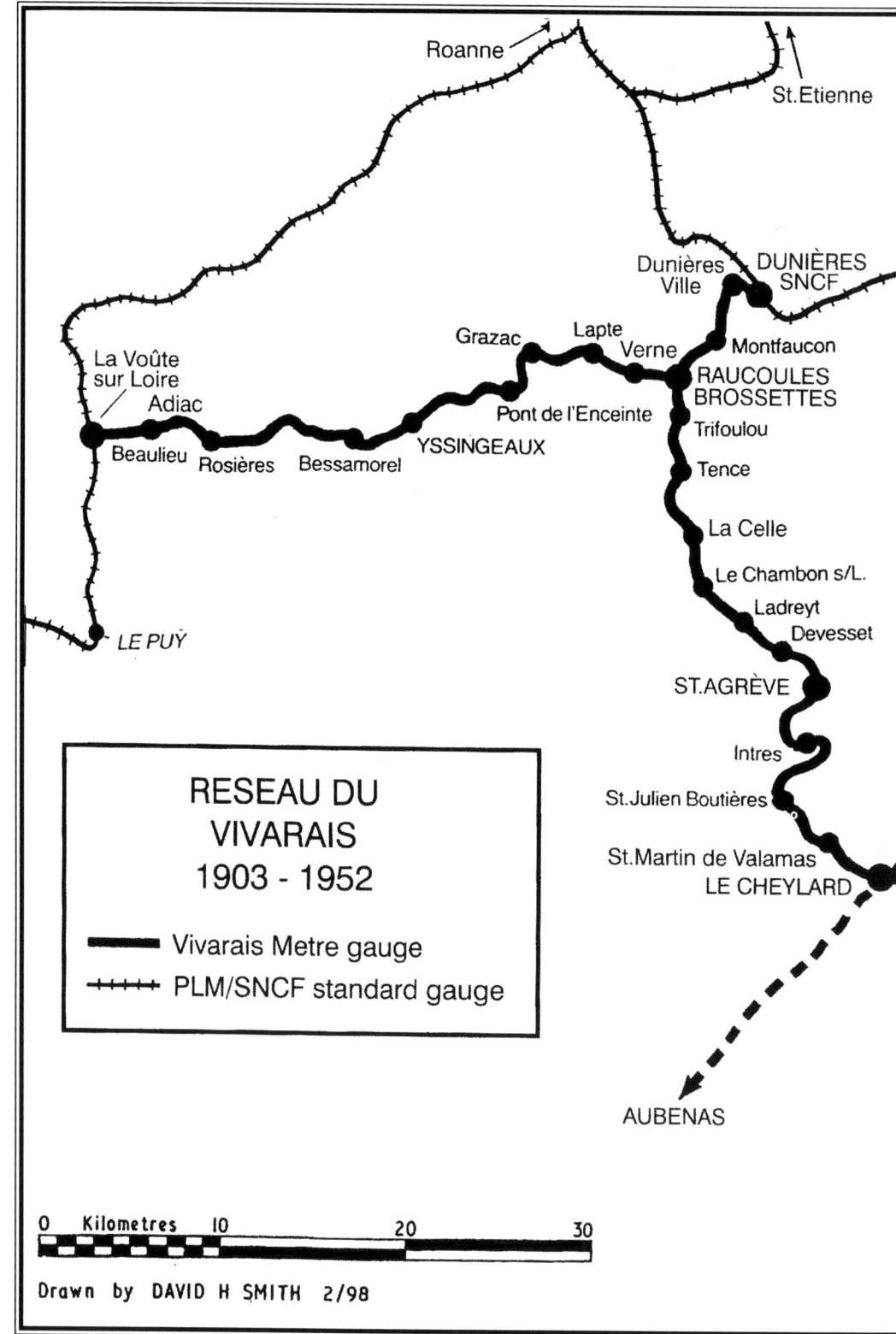

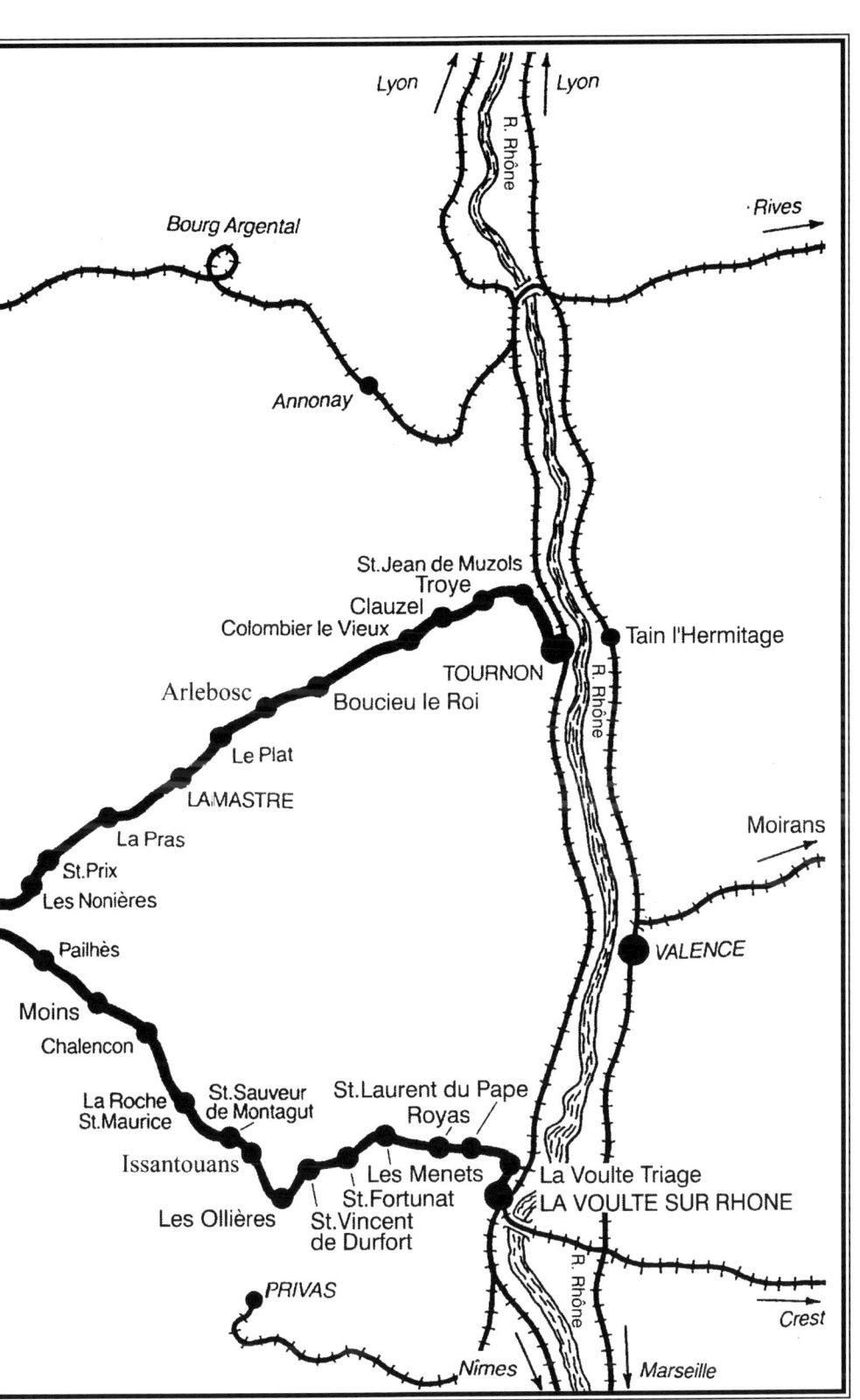

PROFILE OF LINE LA VOULTE SUR RHÔNE to DUNIÈRES

Originally drawn by B. Canet
English version by J.A. Wood

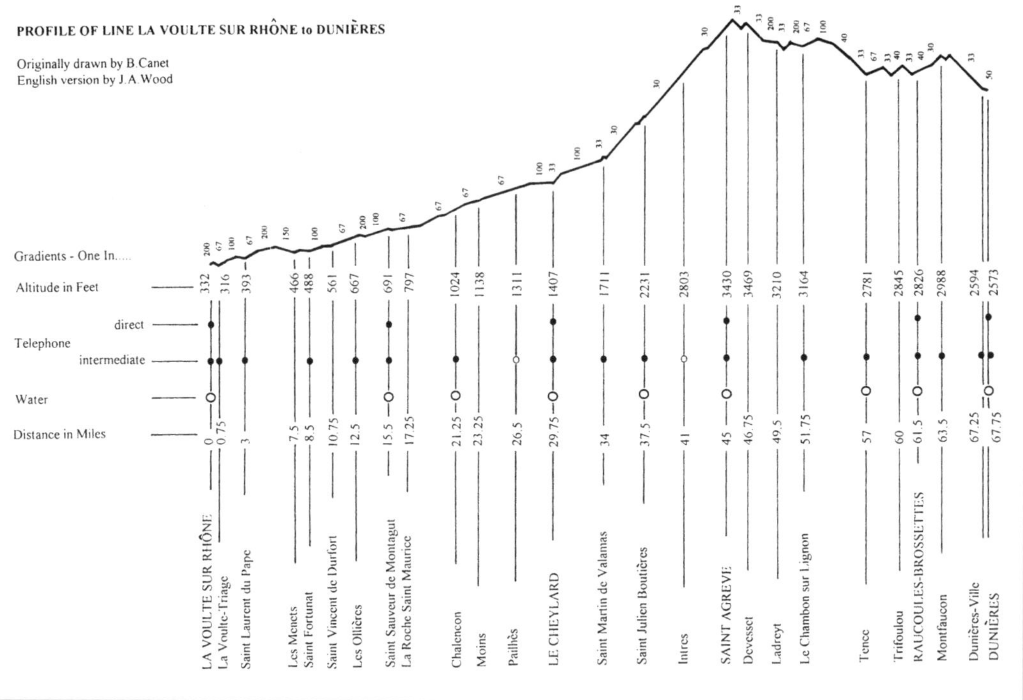

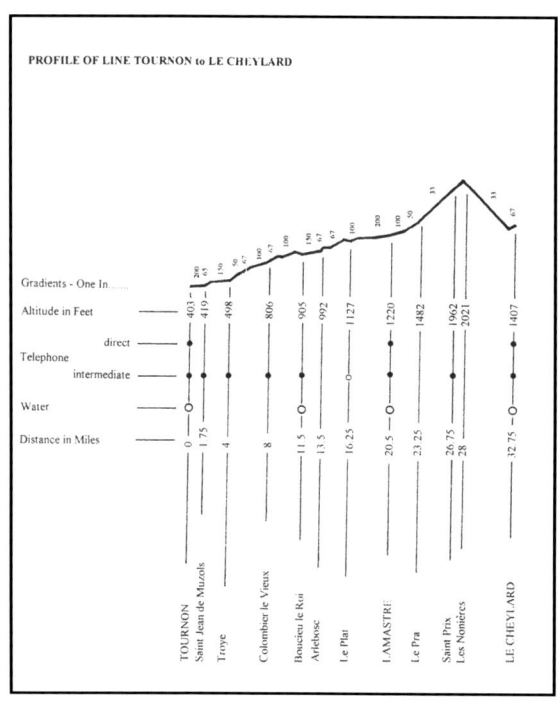

PROFILE OF LINE TOURNON to LE CHEYLARD

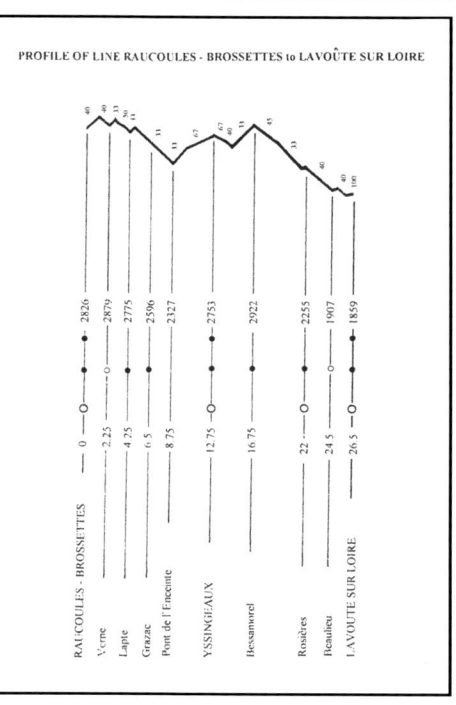

PROFILE OF LINE RAUCOULES - BROSSETTES to LAVOÛTE SUR LOIRE

Following the formation of the Chemin de Fer Départementaux (CFD) in 1881, this company was responsible for the construction and operation of numerous minor railways (Secondaires) throughout France. Many of these were quite substantial undertakings supported by the State and were known as Intérét Générale, whilst others were purely local operations known as Intérét Local. The entire operation was controlled from the CFD head office in Paris, although the individual railways normally operated independently. There was a certain amount of transfer of locomotives and rolling stock, particularly during the 1950s following the closure of a number of the CFD lines.

The Réseau du Vivarais was constructed by the CFD in stages between 1886 and 1903, and ultimately connected the Loire and Rhône Valleys by a highly scenic 202km(126miles) metre gauge route which traversed the Vivarais Mountains in the Massif Central. The various sections of this Intérét Générale system were opened as follows:

La Voûte sur Loire to Yssingeaux (22km/14mls) - 9th November 1890
Tournon to Lamastre (33km/20mls) - 12th July 1891
La Voulte sur Rhône to Le Cheylard (47.5km/30mls) - 10th September 1891
Yssingeaux to Raucoules-Brossettes and Dunières (29km/18mls) - 21st September 1902
Raucoules-Brossettes to St.Agrève (26km/16mls) - 27th September 1902
Le Cheylard to St.Julien Boutières (12.5km/8mls) - 7th December 1902
St.Julien Boutières to St.Agrève (12km/7.5mls) - 29th May 1903
Lamastre to Le Cheylard (20km/12.5mls) - 7th July 1903

For a total of 78 years, the Réseau du Vivarais operated a regular service of passenger and freight trains throughout the area. The major freight transport was timber, much of it destined for the coal mines around St. Etienne where it was used as pit-props. The peak year for the operation of the railway in terms of passenger numbers and freight tonnage was 1913. During that year it transported 664,000 passengers and 170,000 tons of goods. With such figures to satisfy their accountants, the CFD seriously considered extending the line from Le Cheylard to Aubenas during the 1920s. Sadly, this ambitious scheme was never achieved – it would certainly have been an arduous 48km(30miles) route across a mountainous region.

The railway continued to prosper during the 1920s, with a record number of 680,000 passengers being carried in 1929. However with an increase in operating costs and higher wages for the staff, the 1930s were to see a downward trend in overall revenue. Additionally, other means of transport were beginning to have an adverse effect on the traffic receipts. This trend was reversed during World War II, as a result of restrictions on the use of private vehicles and fuel shortages. With the onset of peace in 1945, the use of private cars and commercial road vehicles began to accelerate rapidly, which seriously affected the CFD operation. Despite the increased use of railcars for an accelerated passenger service, the system was beginning to suffer from the competition provided by road transport.

The period during World War II saw the railway engaged in smuggling arms and ammunition for the Resistance, which were hidden within the contents of coal trucks before being stored at a secret hideaway deep in the Doux Gorge. Le Cheylard depot was seriously damaged by a bombardment in 1944 when the advancing American army from the South incorrectly assumed it was of vital importance to the occupying forces!

During the immediate post-war years, the section from La Voûte sur Loire to Raucoules-Brossettes was found to be completely unprofitable, with a mere 22p earned in revenue for every £1.00 spent in operation. Not surprisingly this was a situation that could not be allowed to continue, with the result that this section of the system was closed on 29th February 1952. The remaining 162kms(101miles) remained open, with additional railcars transferred from the recently closed CFD Charentes. Despite continually falling receipts, the CFD Vivarais continued to operate into the 1960s and outlived many of the other minor railways throughout France. The system finally closed on 31st October 1968, when the last railcars made their way through the superb scenery of the Ardèche and Haute-Loire draped in black cloth. As will be seen in a later chapter, this was fortunately not the end of the story.

1.1. With passengers in Edwardian era costume, SLM Mallet no.403 and three Lorraine Dietrich carriages were photographed at St. Agrève during the 1960s. (J.F.Organ coll.)

1.2. The last surviving Fives-Lille 2-6-0T, no.61, was captured during shunting operations at Le Cheylard on 4th August 1954. Numerous examples of this type of locomotive, many of which were also constructed by Cail, were in use throughout France during the first half of the 20th century. (F.Collardeau)

1.3.   During the final year of the CFD operation of the Réseau Vivarais, B-B Diesel Hydraulic locomotive no.040-003 was recorded hauling an empty freight train through the dramatic Doux Gorge on 16th April 1968. (F.Collardeau)

1.4.   Mallet no.403 and one of the Billard type A-150-D-2 articulated railcars were photographed at St.Agrève on 25th July 1966. The passenger stock in the background was stabled at the station during the weekdays, in readiness for the Sunday evening steam hauled service to Dunières. (J.L.Rochaix)

1.5. Sadly the steeply graded and highly scenic route between Le Cheylard and St.Agrève is now a sandy footpath. Intres Viaduct is one of the more accessible reminders of the route. When it was viewed in September 1992, the road had been re-aligned to pass alongside the structure. Originally the road passed through the two arches at each end of the viaduct. (J.F.Organ)

      The Réseau du Vivarais system traversed some extremely hostile and demanding terrain, some of which were amongst the most dramatic and scenic sections of railway in Europe. The eastern and western extremities, where the branches terminated in the valleys of the Rhône and Loire, included long climbs through the gorges of the Rivers Doux and Eyrieux from Tournon and La Voulte, both situated on the Rhône, and the Lignon from La Voûte sur Loire. By contrast the northern section crossed a high plateau, the highest point of which was the 1060m watershed of the Atlantic and Mediterranean. This summit near St.Agrève also formed the boundary of the Dèpartements of the Haute-Loire and Ardèche. St.Agrève was connected to the principle junction and headquarters at Le Cheylard by the most dramatic section of the system, which included a series of viaducts and tunnels combined with steep gradients of up to 1 in 30 through the upper reaches of the Eyrieux Gorge. Main line connections were made at La Voûte sur Loire, Tournon, La Voulte sur Rhône and Dunières. Those at Tournon and La Voulte sur Rhône were notable for their sections of dual gauge track, where the metre gauge Vivarais rails were interlaced with those of the PLM (now SNCF) route between Lyon and Nimes.

      Fortunately, thanks to the efforts of the CFV and VFV, two very contrasting sections of the system are still in use. These are the scenically impressive route through the Doux Gorge between Tournon and Lamastre, whilst the line across the high plateau between Dunières and St.Agrève provides a completely different aspect of the Vivarais topography. The steeply graded and arduous route between Le Cheylard and St.Agrève is now largely passable as an interesting footpath, whilst part of the Le Cheylard to Lamastre line has been converted into a minor road. The large loco-shed and workshop at Le Cheylard is still in use – as a bus depot!

1.6.   No.403 awaits departure from Les Ollières with a FACS special between Le Cheylard and La Voulte sur Rhône on 11th May 1963. Note the improvised "headboard" chalked on the smoke-box of the locomotive. (Colour-Rail)

1.7.   SLM Mallet no.404 was recorded outside the extensive depot at Le Cheylard on 21st July 1962. This building is still in use as a bus depot! (D.Trevor Rowe)

1.8. Billard type A-150-D railcar no.212 was viewed at St.Martin de Valamas, whilst working a passenger service between Le Cheylard and Dunières on 21st July 1962. This was a typical example of passenger working during the final 30 years of the Vivarais under CFD control. *(D.Trevor Rowe)*

1.9. Whilst hauling another FACS special, from Tournon to Dunières, no.403 replenished its water tanks at Boucieu le Roi whilst a Billard railcar stood alongside. This almost timeless view is from 8th May 1966. *(D.Trevor Rowe)*

1.10. The same train was recorded about to depart from Les Nonières. Note the tank wagon behind the locomotive as reserve water supply. No.403 was fitted with a primitive spark arrestor to the chimney, a notable feature of the Vivarais locomotives during the CFD era. (D.Trevor Rowe)

1.11. The FACS special halts at the spacious station at Le Cheylard, before commencing the steep climb to St.Agrève. The B-B Diesel Hydraulic locomotive no. 040-003 can be seen in the background. (D.Trevor Rowe)

1.12.   Another water stop for the FACS special train on 8th May 1966. This time the location is Tence, which is now the principal intermediate station of the VFV tourist operation. (D.Trevor Rowe)

1.13.   The last steam hauled train to operate on the Vivarais during the CFD era was chartered by the British based Continental Railway Circle. No.403, now wearing its recently applied green livery, is ready to depart from Tournon with the special train in September 1968. (Colour-Rail)

1.14.   During a later stage of the CRC tour, a photo-stop was made at the rural station of Raucoules-Brossettes prior to the final descent to Dunières. By that period, with closure only weeks away, nature was already beginning to reclaim the track at this exposed location. (Colour-Rail)

1.15.   At the completion of its 114km (71 miles) journey, a travel stained no.403 was turned at Dunières depot whilst still proudly carrying its CRC headboard and the British and French flags. This was truly the end of an era, fortunately to be shortly followed by the beginning of another period of Vivarais history. (Colour-Rail)

CFD de la LOZÈRE 1909-1968

Although the CFD lines were normally operated independently of each other, a notable exception was the Lozère line. This 48km(30miles) metre gauge railway was always operated as an isolated branch of the Vivarais, with a regular transfer of locomotives and railcars from Le Cheylard throughout its history. Situated in the Cèvennes, about 100km(60miles) south of the main Vivarais network, this highly scenic line connected Florac with the equally scenic former PLM route, linking Clermont-Ferrand and Nimes, at Ste. Cécile D'Andorge.

This curvaceous and steeply graded line was opened in 1909, with its headquarters and principal depot established at Florac. As with the parent Vivarais system, timber was one of the major items of freight carried. However, unlike the Vivarais where full-length tree trunks were carried on double flat trucks, the Lozère transported timber in short lengths stacked in open high-sided wagons. Railcars were introduced for passenger services during the 1930s, whilst the last remaining steam locomotives were replaced by diesel powered machines during the early 1950s.

The route of this interesting railway climbed from Florac, in the shadow of the Causse Mejean Massif, via a series of ledges above the River Mimente, a tributary of the Tarn, to a summit tunnel beneath the 832m Col de Jalcreste. The line then descended via a tortuous route above the valley of the River Gardon, a tributary of the Gard, before arriving at Ste.Cécile D'Andorge across a curving six arched viaduct. This much loved railway suffered in much the same way as its contemporaries during the post World War II period with competition from road transport. The Lozère line was closed on 1st April 1968, the remaining diesel locomotives and railcars ultimately being transferred to Le Cheylard or Dunières. The following year a proposed scheme to operate steam hauled tourist trains was announced. This scheme failed to attract sufficient interest and finance to be a viable proposition. No doubt the two preservation schemes that began to evolve on the Vivarais system at the same time attracted more support, largely due to their more convenient locations.

1.16. Florac was the headquarters and terminus of the CFD de la Lozère. De Dion Bouton type ND railcar no.201 was recorded prior to departing with a service bound for St.Cécile d'Andorge on 23rd July 1962. (D.Trevor Rowe)

1.17. During the course of its journey, no.201 halts at St. Privat-de-Vallongue, whilst another De Dion type ND railcar and its single axle trailer stands alongside. Note the boxes of merchandise loaded onto the trailer vehicle. (D.Trevor Rowe)

1.18. The CFD de la Lozère approached the main line connection at St.Cécile d'Andorge via this curved viaduct, which crossed the valley of the River Gardon, a tributary of the River Gard. The viaduct was viewed on 23rd July 1962. (D.Trevor Rowe)

───────→ *1.19. At the completion of its journey from Florac, De Dion railcar no.201 was recorded in the headshunt at St.Cécile d'Andorge on the far side of the SNCF tracks. (D.Trevor Rowe)*

───────→ *1.20. The SNCF is seen from the CFD de la Lozère platform at St.Cécile d'Andorge. Class 141E 2-8-2s, nos 566 and 430, were recorded departing with a train bound for Clermont Ferrand on 22nd July 1962. (D.Trevor Rowe)*

1.21. *A classic view of the Lozère line during its final years of operation features CFD loco-tractor no.62 at Rouve-Jalcreste, whilst hauling a freight train loaded with timber bound for St.Cécile d'Andorge on 22nd April 1965. (J-L.Rochaix)*

TRAMWAYS DE L'ARDÈCHE

In addition to the CFD metre gauge lines in the Ardèche and Haute-Loire, this independent short lived Intérét Local system was situated south of the Vivarais network. With its headquarters at Privas, the line ran from the west-bank of the Rhône at Le Pouzin to St.Paul-le-Jeune, a distance of 104km (65 miles) to the south west. Principal intermediate stations were established at Privas, Aubenas and Les Vans.

Constructed during the first decade of the 20th century, this lightly laid basic tramway operated for a mere 20 years between 1910 and 1930. Motive power was provided by a small array of Piguet 2-6-0Ts, similar to the CFD Fives-Lille and Cail locomotives. Traffic figures never lived up to expectations, the operation being transferred to road transport when the operating concession expired in 1930.

Part 2 - VIVARAIS AND LOZÈRE LOCOMOTIVES AND RAILCARS

Steam Locomotives

Between 1890 and 1932, the CFD supplied a total of 33 steam locomotives for use on the Réseau du Vivarais, plus an additional two which were supplied directly to the CFD de la Lozère. Within a short period of time, three locomotives were transferred from Le Cheylard to Florac on a permanent basis, whilst a further six locomotives from the Vivarais stock were transferred to the Lozère line for shorter periods throughout the life of the two railways.

The first locomotives were six 0-4-4-0T compound Mallets built by Société Alsacienne de Constructions Mécaniques (SACM) Belfort in 1890/1. As with all the locomotives supplied to the two lines, these carried CFD numbers, being nos 45-48 and 63-64. No.48 was sold to the CF Provence in 1943 and no.64 was based at Florac between 1916 and 1919. The last of these small Mallets, no.63, was withdrawn from service in 1946, but surprisingly remained in store until 1965.

The small Mallets were joined in 1891 by six 2-6-0Ts from Fives-Lille, nos 57-62, for use on the less heavily graded sections of the route. These locomotives served the Vivarais well, particularly on the La Voulte – Le Cheylard line with its less demanding gradients. No.62 was transferred to CFD Charentes in 1914, whilst nos 57,58 and 60 were casualties of war when they were damaged beyond repair during the bombardment of Le Cheylard in 1944. The last survivor was no.61, which was withdrawn in 1957 although it remained in store until 1965.

Whilst the steeply graded sections between Le Cheylard and Dunières were being constructed in 1902, three Pinguely 0-6-0Ts, nos 81 –83, were acquired for use on construction trains. These had all been transferred elsewhere within the CFD group by 1909. However, no.81 was drafted to Florac in that year, followed by no.82 for a short period during 1929 and 1930. Only no.81 remained at Florac for any appreciable time, interspersed with periods elsewhere in France, including a return to Le Cheylard between 1923 and 1928. It was finally withdrawn around the time of WWII.

For operation on the completed Vivarais network after 1903, far more powerful locomotives were required. The result was the class of locomotive for which the Vivarais has become most renowned. These were the eight 0-6-6-0T compound Mallets supplied by Schweizerische Locomotiv und Maschinenfabrik (SLM) between 1902 and 1905, nos 401-408. These powerful locomotives were more than equal for the tasks demanded of them, being capable of hauling heavy freight trains up the reverse curves of the 1 in 30 gradients unassisted. Apart from no.402, which was withdrawn in 1942 and eventually scrapped in 1955, all survived in service until the 1960s. No.408 was based at Florac between 1909 and 1911, whilst no.406 was loaned to the CF Provence during 1944-45. Nos 401, 403 and 404 were secured for preservation by the CFV and based at Tournon.

In 1906, a Fives-Lille compound 2-6-2T, no.251, was supplied for use on the La Voulte - Le Cheylard route. Although this locomotive proved unpopular with the Vivarais crews, it was transferred to Florac in 1909 where it remained in use until 1949 – apart from a period of war service in Northern France during World War I.

SACM Belfort supplied five 2-4-4-0T compound Mallets in 1908, principally for use on passenger trains. Nos 321–323 were delivered to Le Cheylard, whilst nos 324-325 went to Florac. No.323 was transferred to the Lozère in 1911, whilst no.322 also spent the last decade of its life between 1945 and 1956 based at Florac. Both nos 321 and 322 were loaned to the Provence line during 1944-5. All five locomotives were withdrawn by or during the 1950s, although nos 324 and 325 remained in store at Florac for a further decade until they were finally scrapped in 1964.

The last steam locomotives supplied to the CFD Vivarais were the six 0-6-6-0T Mallets constructed by SACM Graffenstaden. These had almost identical power bogies to the earlier Swiss built machines, but were fitted with larger and higher pitched Belpaire boilers. The first two, nos 409-410, were delivered to Le Cheylard in 1927. These were followed by a further four similar locomotives, with improved cabs and coal bunkers, in 1932 - nos 411-414. This final batch of Mallets has earned its place in history as being the last metre gauge locomotives built in France for use in that country. Nos 409 and 410 were transferred to Florac between 1932 and 1942. Due to their higher centre of gravity, these later machines proved to be less popular with the crews than the earlier Swiss locomotives. The majority were withdrawn in 1955, apart from nos 413 and 414. These remained in store at Le Cheylard until 1968 and were ultimately preserved for use on the newly formed CFV. The previous concerns about their stability having been overcome, these two Mallets, with their larger fuel and water capacity, have proved to be an invaluable asset to the tourist operation.

2.1.   Although none of the CFD Fives-Lille 2-6-0Ts survived into the preservation era, a Cail example of the same design has been restored for service on the CF de la Baie de Somme in Northern France. This locomotive was built in 1889 for use on the Panama Canal construction railway and subsequently spent much of its life in the USA. Following repatriation in 1994, no.2 has undergone an extensive restoration and was photographed at Le Crotoy on 16th September 2006. (J.F.Organ)

2.2.   Arguably the most famous locomotives to have worked on the CFD Vivarais were the eight SLM 0-6-6-0T Mallets, nos 401-408. One of the three surviving members of the class, no.403, was viewed at Tournon depot in September 1998, shortly after it had re-entered service following a major overhaul. (J.F.Organ)

2.3.   Sister locomotive no.404 was recorded whilst being turned at Lamastre on 17th September 1989. Note the modified cab incorporating a small fuel bunker. No.404 was one of four SLM Mallets to receive this modification shortly after World War II, in an attempt to increase their operational capabilities. (J.F.Organ)

2.4.   One of the four SACM Mallets supplied in 1932, no.413 was recorded as it was about to depart from Colombier le Vieux with a Tournon bound train in September 1992. The larger higher pitched boiler of these later machines is very apparent in this view of the locomotive. (J.F.Organ)

2.5.   SACM 0-6-6-0T Mallet no.414 was the last metre gauge locomotive to be supplied for use in France, although later machines were constructed for export contracts. This historic locomotive was photographed collecting a freight wagon from St. Jean-de-Muzols on 26th March 2005. (F.Mottet)

Diesel Locomotives

Following World War II, the CFD had a surplus of smaller locomotives that required complete rebuilds. Rather than incur the cost of replacement boilers, the CFD overhauled the frames and wheels of these machines and fitted them with diesel power units. This resulted in some powerful locomotives that were equally at home hauling freight trains or for shunting duties. The majority were constructed at the CFD workshops at Montmirail, east of Paris, whilst others were converted at the workshops of the individual railways.

The pioneer diesel locomotive constructed at Montmirail in 1946 was based on a Couillet 0-6-2T from the CFD Seine et Marne. Fitted with a 180hp Willème diesel power unit, no.852 was tested at Le Cheylard before returning to its original line. Following the successful testing of no.852, the workshops at Le Cheylard undertook the conversion of two St.Léonard 0-6-2Ts dating from 1887, originally supplied to the CFD l'Yonne. These were converted into diesel powered 0-6-0s, utilising the excellent 8-cylinder Willème 180hp power unit. Known as loco-tractors X and Y, these versatile machines took over many of the duties formerly undertaken by the smaller steam locomotives. In addition to shunting operations, they were often to be seen hauling some of the lighter freight trains, particularly on the La Voulte line. Both survived in service until 1968 and have been preserved by the CFV at Tournon.

Between 1960 and 1968, X and Y were joined at Le Cheylard by another similar machine. This was no.13, which had previously worked on the CFD Seine et Marne. No.13 was rebuilt in 1946 from a Couillet 0-6-0T originally supplied to the S&M in 1883. Unlike the other loco-tractors, it was fitted with a slightly less powerful 150hp Willème power unit.

The Lozère received two similar locomotives converted at Montmirail in 1946 and 1948. These were nos 62 and 70, both originating as 2-6-0Ts on the CFD Charentes system. No.62 was rebuilt from a Fives-Lille machine, which had originally been a Vivarais locomotive until 1914, whilst no.70 was converted from a similar Cail example. In addition, an earlier conversion derived from a SACM Belfort 2-6-0T, no.50, was based for a short period at Florac during 1951. Nos 62 and 70 hauled the majority of the freight traffic on the Lozère during the final two decades of the line's existence, and survived into preservation. They are now based at Tence, where they handle a high proportion of the VFV tourist traffic.

In 1954, the Vivarais acquired a small petrol powered 4w loco-tractor. This diminutive machine, built by Pétolat, had been originally supplied to the CF Saône et Loire in 1930 and was powered by a 12hp Daimler engine. This was used for light shunting duties around the depot at Le Cheylard until 1968. It was saved for preservation by the CFV and was put in store at Lamastre.

The final diesel powered locomotive to arrive at Le Cheylard was in a very different league. In 1962/3, the CFD works at Montmirail constructed four powerful B-B Diesel Hydraulic machines. These 32 tonne 400hp locomotives were fitted with two, Poyaud 6 cylinder power units. They were equipped with a high central cab, similar to many standard gauge locomotives of the same era. The first two were supplied to the State owned PO Corrèze (POC), whilst another went to Corsica. No.040-003 was supplied to Le Cheylard in October 1963 with the intention of it working alongside the remaining Mallets on freight haulage. Such was the success of this modern locomotive, it did in fact handle the majority of the freight traffic during the final years of the CFD Vivarais operation.

Following the closure of the Vivarais in 1968, no.040-003 was sold to the CF Provence, where it was ultimately joined by the two "sister" locomotives from the POC. The latter machines were destined to remain in Provence, whilst no.040-003 was transferred to Corsica in 1974.

Railcars

The CFD had tested various petrol engine vehicles on many of its lines during the 1920s, most of which were deemed to be under-powered for their intended purposes. However, by the 1930s, diesel power units had been developed to a point where they had become a viable means of propulsion. Consequently, some of the well-known motor vehicle manufacturers realised that there were new business opportunities to be achieved from branching out into the light railway market.

The first railcars (or Autorails as they are known in France) supplied to the CFD for use in the Ardèche and Haute-Loire were seven single ended vehicles constructed by De Dion Bouton in 1935. These were De Dion type ND machines, nos 201-207 and were powered by a 100hp Mercedes engine, built under licence by Unic. The power units were mounted directly above a power bogie at the front of the vehicle, the rear of the railcar being carried on a single trailing axle. Being single ended, they relied upon having to be turned at each end of their journeys – fortunately the Vivarais and, to a lesser extent, the Lozère were both equipped with numerous turntables. However, these vehicles were also equipped with a built-in jack/turning device should the need arise to turn them at a location devoid of a turntable.

Nos 201 and 202 were allocated to Florac, where they spent their entire working lives. The remainder were initially sent to Le Cheylard, although nos 204 and 205 were transferred to the Lozère at various times between 1938 and 1968. No.204 is the lone working survivor, based on the VFV, whilst no.207 is in store at Lamastre. Nos 201,202 and 206 "survived" in a derelict condition at Raucoules-Brossettes, no.202 being sold to the Musée des Transports a Vapeur et des Chemins de Fer Secondaires Francais (MTVS) near Paris in 2002 as a long term restoration project.

The railcars most commonly associated with the Vivarais were the four Billard Type A-150-D units supplied in1938 and 1940. These double-ended vehicles, nos 211-214 proved to be an instant success with their flexibility of operation. The power unit was mounted directly above the leading end power bogie, whilst the rear bogie was a purely trailing unit. Initially, nos 211-213 were fitted with 150hp CLM diesel engines, whilst 214 was fitted with a Berliet motor of similar size. During the 1940s, these motors were all replaced by the more efficient and reliable 150hp 6-cylinder Willème power units.

All four vehicles provided excellent service to the Vivarais until 1968, whilst no.214 was based at Florac between 1961 and 1967. Nos 211 and 212 were sold to the CF Provence in 1969, no.211 ending its days with its trailing end adapted as the cab of a manned snowplough! Nos 213 and 214 were more fortunate, being preserved for use on the CFV.

In 1939, Société Anonyme Billard supplied a further four units to the CFD for use on the Vivarais. These were the Articulated Type A-150-D-2 variants, nos 221 –224. Basically, these were comprised of two of the smaller Billard A-80-D units permanently coupled together with their trailing end driving positions removed. They were mounted on three bogies, the centre one being positioned under both vehicles. The power unit was positioned in the rear of the leading car, connected to the centre bogie. As with the other Billard railcars, the original CLM engines were replaced by 150hp Willème power units at an early stage of their lives. These advanced vehicles were highly regarded on the Vivarais. During the late 1940s they were used on a short lived non-stop service between La Voulte sur Rhône and Dunières, which carried the name Flèche des Cèvennes. Sadly this innovate service was introduced too late to stem the rapidly diminishing number of passengers on the route.

Following the closure of the Vivarais in 1968, nos 223 and 224 were sold to the Provence line, whilst no.222 is the sole survivor. This is in fact a combination of nos 221 and 222, the former having been withdrawn in 1955 following an accident. No.222 is now in service on the VFV, being based at St.Agrève.

After the CFD Charentes line was closed in 1952, four smaller Billard Type A-80-D units were transferred to Le Cheylard. Nos 313-316 proved to be invaluable for the lighter passenger services. They were basically a scaled down version of the A-150-D design, supplied in 1937/8 and originally fitted with 90hp CLM engines. These were changed to the 100hp 4-cylinder Willème units early in their lives. No.314 was transferred to Florac between 1954-61, and again from 1967. All four have survived, nos 314 and 316 in the care of the CFV whilst no.313 is in service on the VFV. No.315 remains in a derelict condition at Dunières, having been used as a source of spare parts.

In 1932 Campagne à Paris supplied a small petrol powered track inspection vehicle (Draisine) utilising Citroen components. This small machine (no.1) was joined by another of the same type in 1952, no.2 arriving from Charentes at the same time as the A-80-D railcars from the same source. Both have survived with the CFV, and are currently based at Lamastre.

2.6. CFD- Le Cheylard built loco-tractor "Y" was recorded at Tournon depot alongside Billard typeR-210 trailer car no.3 and Billard type A-150-D railcar no.213 on 15th August 2006. (P.Barnes)

2.7. CFD-Montmirail loco-tractor no.70, formerly based at Florac, was viewed outside the VFV rolling stock shed at Tence on 10th September 2006. The carriage in the background is one of two constructed by the VFV on the chassis of a freight wagon. (J.F.Organ)

2.8. One of the De Dion Bouton type ND railcars was recorded at Florac on 9th July 1962. Being single ended, these earlier railcars lacked the versatility of the later double ended Billard designs. (J-L. Rochaix)

2.9. The superb Billard type A-150-D railcar no.213 was photographed at Lamastre, prior to working an afternoon service to Tournon, in June 1994. The delivery of the four A-150-D machines between 1938 and 1940 revolutionised the passenger services on the Vivarais system. (J.Marsh)

2.10. Articulated Billard A-150-D-2 railcar no. 222 is pictured at Raucoules-Brossettes shortly before entering service on the VFV, following an overhaul, on 28th August 1996. These high capacity vehicles were another successful innovation following their delivery in 1939. *(J.F.Organ)*

2.11. One of the former CFD Charentes Billard A-80-D railcars, no. 314, was recorded at Lamastre in September 1998. These smaller vehicles were used extensively on lighter services, after their transfer to the Vivarais in 1952. *(J.F.Organ)*

Part 3 - ROLLING STOCK OF THE CFD VIVARAIS

A large number of passenger and freight vehicles were supplied to the CFD for use on their two lines in the Ardèche/Haute-Loire and Cévennes. Between 1890 and 1932, a total of 49 carriages of various types were supplied to the Vivarais, whilst a further 10 went to the Lozère. In addition a large number of freight wagons of many variations were supplied to both lines.

Carriages

The first passenger vehicles to be supplied for use on the initial sections of the Vivarais in 1890/1 were 23 bogie carriages built by La Buire. These comprised of 12 3rd class and 11 composites. These fairly basic vehicles were built to the classic "bow-sided" design, only the 1st class compartments offering any degree of comfort.

These were followed in 1902 by a further 11 similar carriages built by De Dietrich, including three composites and eight 3rd class examples. Four composites of a similar design from Decauville were supplied to the Lozère in 1909, followed a short time later by six 3rd class saloons from the same manufacturer.

In 1902, De Dietrich also supplied a palatial 4-wheeled "Directors Saloon". This elegant carriage included an open saloon with an end balcony and a well-appointed compartment, which were separated by a toilet and a small dining area. Two years later, De Dietrich supplied a further four small carriages, which like the saloon were 4 wheeled vehicles. Two were 2nd /3rd class composites, including a guards compartment incorporating a "birdcage" look-out on the roof, whilst the other pair were basic 3rd class vehicles. Due to their small size and relatively high seating capacity, these were known as "Henhouses".

After the delivery of the 4-wheeled carriages in 1904, no further passenger vehicles were supplied until 1927. In that year Lorraine Deitrich supplied some of the most elegant and sumptuous carriages supplied for use on a narrow gauge railway. These steel bodied bogie vehicles were supplied in two batches, six 3rd class examples being supplied in 1927 followed by four 1st /2nd class composites in 1931. Both variations incorporated a combination of corridor and open saloon accommodation, whilst the composites were also equipped with a toilet. The external design of these advanced carriages featured angled inset doors and tapered roof ends, not unlike the design adopted in 1935 by the GWR for their "Centenary Stock". Similar Italian built carriages were also supplied to Portugal in 1931.

After the arrival of these advanced vehicles, followed a short time later by the first railcars, many of the earlier carriages were either transferred elsewhere within the CFD, or were shorn of their bodywork and converted into flat wagons.

Luggage Vans

In addition to the passenger carrying vehicles, a large number of luggage vans (or fourgons) were supplied for use with passenger trains as guards vans, in addition to their luggage and parcel capacity. A total of 32 of these four-wheeled vans were supplied by both La Buire and De Dietrich between 1890 and 1927, although ten of the earliest examples were transferred to other CFD lines between 1905 and 1908. Some of the earlier fourgons, which remained at Le Cheylard or Florac, had their guard's compartments removed and converted into goods vans.

Railcar Trailers

In 1938, following the introduction of the Billard A-150-D railcars, three Type R-210 trailer cars were supplied from Tours. Nos 1-3 were basically engine-less A-80-D railcars incorporating a luggage area in place of the engine and drivers compartment.

When the four A-80-D railcars were transferred from Charentes in 1952, they were joined by a further three R-210 trailer cars from the same source, nos 11, 22 and 33. These later arrivals had the luxury of a toilet in place of some of the luggage space.

Florac also received two railcar trailer cars from Charentes in 1952. These were two De Dion type NE vehicles, confusingly also numbered 1 and 3, which were short 4 wheeled trailers derived from the type ND railcars.

At the same time as the De Dion Type ND railcars were introduced in 1935, they were also supplied with six single axle trailer vehicles. These were simple open trucks, which were provided with a canvas roof supported by a hoop frame. During WWII, some of these primitive vehicles were adapted to carry gas producer plants to generate fuel from coal. This was a short-lived attempt to convert some of the railcars to run on gas, as a result of the wartime oil shortages.

The former Charentes Billard railcars were also supplied with goods trailers, nos 10,20 and 30, originally used on the CFD Indre-et-Loire. Unlike the De Dion examples, these were far more substantial vehicles, the three RM trailers being wooden bodied bogie vehicles with a capacity of two tonnes. As late as 1967, the Le Cheylard workshops constructed a steel-bodied four-wheel trailer (no.40) with the same carrying capacity as the Billard RM series.

Freight Wagons

A total of 470 freight vehicles of various types were supplied for use on the Vivarais and Lozère lines between 1890 and 1927. These ranged from flat trucks, coal wagons, box vans, cattle trucks and bogie timber wagons. The majority of the latter were constructed on the frames of withdrawn passenger vehicles, which had been shorn of their bodies. The freight carrying rolling stock was supplied by a number of manufacturers, including La Buire, De Dietrich, Blanc Misseron, Lorraine Dietrich, Decauville and De Marley. In addition there were service vehicles, including a Decauville breakdown crane and fuel tank wagons.

3.1.   De Dietrich supplied five four wheeled carriages to the CFD for use on the Vivarais between 1902 and 1904. The first was the salubrious Directors Inspection Saloon, in which the CFD hierarchy would have been entertained on their visits to the railway. The saloon was recorded at Lamastre, having been hauled from Tournon as part of a special charter train on 17th September 1989. (J.F.Organ)

3.2. The nine Lorraine Dietrich bogie carriages, constructed in 1927 and 1932, were among the most superior vehicles supplied for use on a narrow gauge railway. The four surviving examples in service on the CFV were photographed at Lamastre in August 1994. In the foreground is no.1609, a 1st/2nd composite, the others all being third class saloons. (J.F.Organ)

⟶ 3.3. The ubiquitous luggage vans (fourgons), have become an indelible aspect of locomotive hauled passenger trains on the French narrow gauge lines. This superbly restored example was viewed at Lamastre on 7th September 2006 prior to being shunted around the carriages. These vehicles are normally marshalled immediately behind the locomotive. (J.F.Organ)

⟶ 3.4. Billard type R-210 trailer car no.22 was recorded inside the rolling stock shed at Tournon on 14th August 2006. These vehicles were basically engine-less A-80-D railcars, this example being one of three inherited from CFD Charentes in 1952. (P.Barnes)

3.5. One of the Billard RM railcar luggage and parcels vans, no.20, was like trailer car no.22 and was transferred from Charentes in 1952. This interesting bogie vehicle was photographed on the SGVA storage and restoration sidings at Boucieu le Roi on 6th September 2006. (J.F.Organ)

3.6. The CFD four-wheeled parcels van no.40, built in 1967, was viewed at Tence on 10th September 2006 awaiting restoration. The large railcar behind the van is the former Réseau Breton Decauville type DXW no.X-232, which is also awaiting restoration. (J.F.Organ)

3.7. A selection of the goods vans that have been lovingly restored by the CFV and SGVA, includes one of the water tank wagons that were used for reserve water supply on some of the final steam hauled special trains of the CFD era. These splendid vehicles were recorded at Lamastre during September 1992. (J.F.Organ)

3.8. A restored open truck and a pair of timber carrying flat wagons were photographed at Tence on 10th September 2006. The VFV inherited a large collection of derelict freight vehicles, which are gradually being restored to their former glory. (J.F.Organ)

Part 4 - LE CHEMIN DE FER DU VIVARAIS

Prior to the closure of the Réseau du Vivarais in 1968, numerous special steam-hauled "last trains" were operated during the late 1960s. The majority of these were organised by the Fédération des Amis des Chemins de Fer Secondaires (FACS), although trains were also chartered by other enthusiast organisations. In fact, the final steam-hauled train between Tournon and Dunières in September 1968 was organised by the British based Continental Railway Circle. The last two working SLM Mallets, nos 403 and 404, were in much demand for these trains. In addition, they were used for the last remaining advertised steam-hauled passenger workings. These were the Sunday evening St.Agrève to Dunières services, which were regularly loaded far in excess of the capacity of a railcar during the summer months. The popularity of these special trains sowed the seeds for the preservation schemes that followed.

During the 1950s and 60s, a group of enthusiasts from the Lyon area had formed an organisation known as the Chemin de Fer Touristique du Meyzieu (CFTM). Among their many diverse activities, this group had gathered together a small collection of 60cm industrial locomotives from around France. In order to operate them, a short roadside tramway had been laid at Meyzieu, on the outskirts of Lyon. However by 1968, the CFTM, under the leadership of their "founding father" Jean Arrivetz, had far more ambitious schemes in mind. During 1957 they had tried unsuccessfully to save the electrified metre gauge Annemasse-Sixt line in the Haute-Savoie. With the imminent closure of the CFD Vivarais system, their thoughts turned to saving at least part of this well loved railway.

Various options were discussed, ranging from modest schemes such as preserving one of the surviving Mallets on a short length of track at Lamastre. Alternatively more ambitious projects such as saving the 52km (33 miles) route between Tournon and Le Cheylard were also considered, the extensive depot and workshops at Le Cheylard offering an ideal headquarters for such an operation. The dramatic and steeply graded line between Le Cheylard and St.Agrève was also examined, this being rejected as being too expensive to operate and maintain.

During September 1968, shortly before the system closed, Jean Arrivetz was at Lamastre examining the track layout and facilities. By coincidence, his visit coincided with that of the French Inspector General of Land Transport, Monsieur Artaud-Macari. Although the railway was due to close, it would remain the property of the State until the CFD lease expired in 1985. Seizing the opportunity, Jean Arrivetz introduced himself to the inspector and outlined the CFTM proposals. Having been invited to join the official party on their return journey to Le Cheylard, Jean Arrivetz was asked to present a detailed plan to Artaud-Macari in Paris the following week.

At that time, railway preservation schemes were virtually unknown in France. However, Jean Arrivetz had visited North Wales earlier that year and was able to produce photographic evidence of tourists and enthusiasts spending vast amounts of money at Portmadoc and Towyn, which impressed both the Parisian politicians and the General Councils of the Ardèche greatly. As a direct result, the CFTM were granted the authority to operate a tourist railway between St Jean de Muzols and Lamastre from 15th June 1969. Access to the dual gauge SNCF track between Tournon and St.Jean de Muzols was denied at that time, whilst the upper section of the route between Lamastre and Le Cheylard was rejected, being considered too expensive to operate and would probably produce very little additional revenue.

With the CFTM now subtly renamed Chemins de Fer Touristiques et de Montagne (Tourist and Mountain Railway Company), they were now the operating company of the Chemin de Fer du Vivarais (CFV). The company took possession of the 31km (19miles) of metre gauge track and sidings, including the extensive layout at Lamastre. To operate the line, the CFTM acquired the five surviving Mallets, five railcars and two diesel loco-tractors. The majority of the surviving passenger carriages were also secured together with four fourgons and a large collection of freight wagons.

Prior to the commencement of the new tourist service, the first train to operate under CFTM auspices was early in June 1969, when railcar no.214 was moved from Le Cheylard to Lamastre. The following month, Mallet no.404 returned to Le Cheylard to collect vans and wagons loaded with much valuable equipment, including hundreds of sleepers and other track fittings. Attached to the rear of this train was De Dion railcar no.207. Despite the sceptics who thought the new regime wouldn't survive a month, the first revenue earning train under CFTM control ran on 22nd June 1969, a week after they officially took possession of the line. This first train, consisting of no.403 hauling four bogie carriages, carried 240 passengers between St.Jean de Muzols and Lamastre. During the remainder of the 1969 season, a total of more than 9,000 passengers were carried, thus convincing the authorities that the operation was a viable proposition. Meanwhile a supporting society was formed, Sauvegarde et Gestion des Vehicules Anciens (SGVA), which provided volunteer working parties to assist with the multitude of outstanding tasks required to bring the CFV up to a suitable standard for attracting the tourist market. Many items of rolling stock have also been restored by the society.

With a more intensive service planned for the following year, it was obvious that additional passenger vehicles would be required. In addition, the two working steam locomotives would require heavy overhauls within a short time. Consequently, the CFTM joined forces with FACS and scoured France and Switzerland for suitable equipment. As a result, the stock was considerably enlarged with the subsequent arrival of additional locomotives and carriages from numerous sources.

With so much activity it was obvious that the new venture was a serious proposition, which the authorities were quick to take note of. As a consequence, early in 1970 the SNCF agreed to the CFV having access to Tournon station and depot, via the 2km of dual gauge track. Although not a cheap option, with an annual fee of over £40,000 for the use of this section of track, the advantages were enormous. Not only was Tournon a more convenient location for the principal terminal station, it also boasted a large engine shed and workshop, turntable, water tower and many sidings for storage of rolling stock. Having obtained the use of the entire route from Tournon to Lamastre, the 1970 season began on 18th April when no.403, proudly flying a *Tricolore*, hauled a train consisting entirely of Vivarais origin, including the Inspection Saloon. Le Mastrou, the local name for the railway – derived from Lamastre, was back with a vengeance. During 1970, 19,000 passengers were carried, which augured well for the future prospects of the fledging organisation.

Despite this initial success, 1970 was not completely trouble free. A landslide in the Doux Gorge caused considerable disruption, largely due to its inaccessibility, whilst an uncharacteristic collision between two railcars was something that the CFV could well have done without! Despite these setbacks, the operation began to prosper and rapidly became one of the most successful of the French tourist railways, carrying over 60,000 passengers annually. When the CFD lease expired in 1985, the CFTM were in a position to take over the ownership of the railway infrastructure and equipment between St.Jean de Muzols and Lamastre. Obviously the dual section at Tournon remained SNCF property, together with its onerous charges.

The railway continued to prosper during the 1970s and 1980s and gained universal recognition of its tremendous efforts in preserving this most spectacular line. In 1991 a twinning arrangement with the Festiniog Railway was announced, thus linking the premier narrow gauge railways of France and Great Britain. Concurrently, CFTM President Jean Arrivetz was appointed as a Patron of the Festiniog Company. He has always freely acknowledged that the early success of the Welsh narrow gauge lines had directly influenced the success of the Vivarais operation.

By the late 1990s, the Lyon based directors of the CFTM were all of increasing age and were looking for another company to operate the railway. During the next three years or so, many negotiations took place with potential interested parties. Ultimately, on 1st January 2004, the ownership of the railway was passed jointly to the Département of Ardèche and a new CFV company based in Tournon. The full name of this company is Chemin de Fer du Vivarais (Société Anonyme d' Economie Mixte Locale). The Council own 51% of the railway, providing much of the finance, whilst the CFV own 49% and provide the staff and equipment to operate the line. As the CFV is the major tourist attraction of the area, the Ardèche Council involvement is a logical step to protect their interests in promoting tourism to this beautiful part of France.

During the course of the negotiations to transfer the ownership of the railway, the CFTM were involved in a potentially serious threat to the continued operation of the CFV. During 2002, the SNCF and RFF (the French equivalent of Network Rail) announced their plans to upgrade the route between Nimes and Lyon as part of a high-speed freight route linking Barcelona and Copenhagen. This work would entail replacing the life expired lattice girder bridge at St.Jean de Muzols with a new structure more compatible with the upgraded line. Initially, the SNCF insisted that the dual gauge section be abandoned, with the CFV operation being terminated beyond the junction at St.Jean de Muzols. Alternatively, the RFF demanded a contribution of 1,000,000 Euros from the CFTM as their contribution towards the cost of the new bridge, should they wish to continue operating into Tournon. This figure was well beyond the means of the CFTM and it looked as though they would have to lose the use of the dual gauge section and the large depot at Tournon. The Ardèche Council agreed to provide 1,600,000 Euros to finance the construction of a new station complex at St.Jean de Muzols, incorporating a fully equipped depot and workshop to replace that likely to be lost at Tournon. Although the high annual charges for the use of the SNCF section would no longer be payable, it was questionable whether such a large sum, needed to construct a new terminus 2km from the centre of Tournon, would be recouped. The Tournon terminus is easily accessible to visitors, whilst the proposed alternative site was certainly far less so.

Following months of protracted negotiations between the various interested parties, the "battle" was finally won in June 2003 following representations to higher government officials. The SNCF agreed to allow the provision of a third rail across the new bridge, whilst the RFF waived its demand for the extortionate contribution towards its construction. Needless to say, the CFV still has to pay the SNCF its annual fee for the use of the dual gauge line, but this is a preferable option than the alternative scheme of an expensive new station at St.Jean de Muzols.

Since the joint regime took control of the operation in 2004, much expenditure has been lavished on improving the railway and its infrastructure. The major outstanding project inherited from the CFTM is the replacement of the life expired track. Originally laid with light rails of 41lb in 24ft lengths, these have lasted remarkably well. There is currently an ongoing scheme to replace these well-worn rails, using heavier section 46 lb/ft rail as much as possible. The locomotives and rolling stock received much overdue maintenance, some items of stock having been stored out of use for some years due to a lack of finance to carry out the necessary work.

With so much activity afoot, the future prospects of the Vivarais operation are very much assured for a continued programme of progress and development.

4.1.   Early morning preparations were in progress when this view was obtained at Tournon depot. From left to right are Billard R-210 trailer no.3, Billard A-80-D no.314, SLM Mallet no.403, SACM Mallet no.413 and former POC Mallet no.104. The scene was recorded prior to the 30th anniversary celebrations of the CFV on 16th July 1999. (J.F.Organ)

4.2.   The Decauville crane, in the company of Loco-Tractor "Y", was about to remove the tanks off Mallet no.414 during September 1998, prior to the locomotives major overhaul. (J.F.Organ)

4.3.   Over five years later the eagerly awaited new boiler for no.414 had arrived from Poland. The partially re-assembled Mallet was recorded being hauled through the depot yard by "Y" on 4th February 2004. (C.Argaud / F.Mottet coll)

4.4.   Awaiting restoration after almost 40 years inactivity, the pioneer SLM Mallet no.401 was recorded in the sidings behind Tournon depot on 12th September 2006. Hopefully, the restoration of this historic locomotive may soon be undertaken by the VFV at Tence. (J.F.Organ)

4.5. Railcar trailer no.3 is hand-shunted into position at Tournon depot, prior to being hauled by railcar no.213 with the evening service to Lamastre on 14th August 2006. (P. Barnes)

The Route - Tournon to Lamastre

The 33km (20miles) line of the CFV is one of many contrasts. It could almost be described as a combination of the best features of the former Réseau du Vivarais, contained in one small section of the original system. The route connects Tournon and Lamastre, both of which are worthy of exploration.

Tournon is a historic town, with its origins dating back to Roman times. The more recent history is notable for it being the home of the 19th Century engineer Marc Seguin. In addition to inventing the water-tube boiler, he also designed a suspension bridge in 1824 that spanned the Rhône at Tournon. Although this historic structure was demolished during the late 1940s, a later suspension bridge dating from 1849 still survives as a footbridge across the river.

Departing from the extensive metre gauge station complex, situated alongside the now closed standard gauge station on the SNCF freight line, the CFV tracks join the dual gauge section of the route via a complex arrangement of switch-less points and track circuiting systems. There immediately follows two tunnels that burrow under the town as the line heads in a northerly direction. Shortly after the second tunnel, the new concrete bridge across the River Doux is crossed before the train slows for another set of switch-less points that lead onto the dedicated metre gauge rails of the Vivarais. The line then curves away towards the level crossing and small station building at St.Jean de Muzols. By now heading in a south-westerly direction, the line runs alongside the road to Douce Plage where one of the major landmarks of the route is situated. This is the large stone built bridge dating from the 15th Century, which at the time of its construction was the largest single-arch bridge in the World.

After passing through the abutments of the bridge, the line now begins the long climb through the Doux Gorge. On the far side of the river can be seen a dam that controls the reservoir for the Tournon water supply. The centre pillar of the dam was constructed from stones that once formed part of a Roman road. The line continues through the Gorge, passing over the river via the curved viaduct at Troye. There then follows the steepest part of the climb, with gradients of up to 1 in 50, leading to Mordane. A hydro-electric power station is located here deep in the gorge, whilst the railway avoids a long curve in the river via a short tunnel. Emerging from the tunnel the halt at Clauzel is passed, where the Resistance stored some of their weapons and ammunition during World War II. On the far side of the gorge can be seen the canal which was constructed by German Prisoners of War during World War I, as part of the Mordane hydro-electric scheme. Now replaced by a pipeline, the concrete construction of the canal bears testimony to this well engineered project, which was built in difficult circumstances. Finally the line veers away from the gorge and draws into one of the two intermediate stations on the line.

Colombier-le-Vieux /St. Barthélémy-le-Plain is situated in an idyllic woodland setting near the river, originally constructed to serve the two villages of the same names, both of which are located some distance away on each side of the valley. The station has been used on many occasions as a film location, including the BBC who used it for the railway sequences in their production of Clochemerle in 1971. After leaving Colombier, the route continues to follow the river, now screened from view by trees, for a further 5.5km (3.5 miles) until the half way station at Boucieu-le-Roi is reached. Here the train stops in order that the locomotive can replenish its water tanks, whilst the passengers partake of some local produce such as wine and cheese. The station has also been adopted by the SGVA as its base, and a number of their items of rolling stock can be seen in the course of restoration.

Departing from Boucieu-le-Roi, the route now adopts a pastoral setting across fields and meadows before crossing the river again at Banchet Viaduct. Overlooking this six-arch structure is a large stone perched precariously on top of a rock outcrop. This is The Turning Stone, which local legend suggests turns every 100 years. However, no one seems to know when it last happened! The river is crossed again at Garnier Viaduct, before the line rejoins the Doux Gorge at Monteil. Shortly after this section above the river, the route crosses the 45th Parallel – mid-way between the North Pole and the Equator. A gentle ascent then leads the line towards Lamastre, which is approached by a roadside section of line along a tree lined avenue.

Lamastre has gained a reputation as a gastronomic centre and is consequently well served by many restaurants and bars. It was the home of the composer Maurice Ravel, in addition to many French personalities from the world of literature.

Upon arrival at Lamastre, the locomotive is turned, its coal bunker and water tanks replenished, before being left to simmer alongside the station whilst the crew and passengers enjoy a leisurely long lunch break. For those wishing to return to Tournon earlier, a railcar often follows the steam hauled train during the peak season and departs again almost immediately. A journey down the line in the front seat of a railcar is considered to be the best way to appreciate the scenic attributes of the CFV. The passengers who wait for the main train will enjoy an afternoon return journey that is invariably more subdued than the outward journey, following the gourmet lunches that many of the passengers have enjoyed!

4.6. Billard A-150-D railcar no.213 and trailer car no.3 were recorded departing from Tournon station during the evening of 14th August 2006. The now closed SNCF station can be seen in the background. (P.Barnes)

4.7. A-150-D railcar no.214 was viewed preparing to depart from Tournon on 24th May 1998. Note the modified front end of this vehicle, which was fitted as a result of accident damage sustained in 1970. (D.Trevor Rowe)

4.8.   Pinguely "Bi-Cabine" 0-6-0T no.31 was photographed departing from Tournon, having joined the SNCF dual gauge section. Unusually, the former CFD inspection saloon is marshalled immediately behind the locomotive for this special charter train on 15th August 2006. (P.Barnes)

4.9.   SACM Mallet no.413 was recorded joining the dual gauge section, upon departure from Tournon, whilst hauling a demonstration mixed train during the 30th anniversary celebrations on 16th July 1999. (J.F.Organ)

4.10. SLM Mallet no.403 was viewed leaving the dual gauge section and joining the dedicated metre gauge track of the CFV at St.Jean-de-Muzols on 17th July 1999. The now demolished lattice-girder viaduct on the SNCF line is visible in the distance. (J.F.Organ)

4.11. A winter scene was recorded at St.Jean-de-Muzols as Billard railcar no 213 passes loco-tractor "X" on 12th December 2006. The siding at this location is a useful refuge for works trains, which avoids their use of the SNCF section. (F.Mottet)

4.12.   Billard no.213 gleams in the evening sun as it approaches Douce Plage, whilst returning to Lamastre during September 1998. The weekday morning and evening railcar services are well patronised by the local residents. (J.F.Organ)

4.13.   The historic bridge at Douce Plage provides an excellent location for viewing the CFV trains in action. No.413 was recorded hauling a Lamastre bound service during September 1998. (J.F.Organ)

4.14.   Railcar no.213 and two trailer cars emerge from the short tunnel through the abutments of Douce Plage bridge, whilst working a morning train to Lamastre in September 1991. (Mrs. B.Organ)

4.15.   Viewed from beneath the arch of the "Grand Pont" at Douce Plage, Billard railcar no.314 was recorded heading towards Lamastre during September 1991. (J.F.Organ)

4.16. No.413 was photographed whilst steadfastly climbing the upper section of the Doux Gorge near Colombier-le-Vieux in September 1992. Note the huge pall of smoke that lingered in the Gorge long after the train had passed. (J.F.Organ)

4.17. SACM Mallet no.413 was photographed hauling a demonstration freight train at Colombier-le-Vieux on 17th July 1999. This view clearly shows how the full-length tree trunks were traditionally carried on two flat trucks, connected by a coupling pole. (J.F.Organ)

4.18.   The delightful setting of the rural station at Colombier-le-Vieux forms a perfect location for this view of Billard no.213 and its trailer, as it pauses briefly whilst en route to Lamastre on the same occasion. (J.F.Organ)

4.19.   Mallet no.414 draws into Boucieu--le-Roi, whilst the tables are set ready with their selection of local produce. These are for the passengers to purchase during the 20 minutes halt at the station, whilst the locomotive replenishes its water supply. (Mrs.B.Organ)

4.20. An elevated view of Boucieu-le Roi station shows no.414 taking water, whilst the passengers enjoy the facilities and refreshments. In the foreground are the SGVA sidings with some of their rolling stock. The framework of De Dietrich bogie carriage no.1427, which is undergoing a long-term restoration, is clearly visible. (P.Barnes)

4.21. During the 1970s, the FACS-owned former Réseau Breton 4-6-0T no.E-327 was loaned to the CFV whilst some of their own locomotives were overhauled. The immaculate locomotive was recorded departing from Boucieu-le-Roi with a train comprised entirely of Breton rolling stock. (SGVA coll.)

4.22. Shortly after departing from Boucieu-le-Roi, SACM Mallet no.414 was recorded passing the level crossing at La Chappelle en-route to Lamastre during August 1994. (J.F.Organ)

4.23. The "turning stone" is clearly visible on the rocky outcrop overlooking the Banchet Viaduct. No.414 is viewed hauling an up train across the viaduct on 6th September 2006. (J.F.Organ)

4.24   No.414 and loco-tractor "Y" were recorded hauling a pre-season maintenance train near Monteil on 9th April 2004. This was one of the first operations for no.414 following an extensive overhaul. (F.Mottet)

4.25.   Pinguely no.31 ascends the final incline on the approach to Lamastre, whilst hauling a permanent way train on 26th April 2005. (F.Mottet)

4.26. In a sylvan setting, railcar no.213 runs into Lamastre station with an evening service from Tournon during August 1994. *(J.F.Organ)*

4.27. SLM Mallet no.403 was photographed as it eased onto the turntable at Lamastre, having just arrived from Tournon on 24th May 1998. *(D.Trevor Rowe)*

4.28. An interesting line-up of motive power was recorded at Lamastre on 9th April 2004. From left to right are loco-Tractor "X", Mallet no.414 and the Billard track maintenance vehicle, no.3, with its attendant tamper. No.3 was converted from a standard gauge railcar in 1957. (F.Mottet)

4.29. Two Monument Historique machines were photographed together at Lamastre on 16th September 2001. SLM Mallet no. 403 was resting during the extended lunch break, whilst Billard A-150-D no.213 was about to return to Lamastre with the early afternoon service. (F.Mottet)

4.30. Prior to the return journey, no.414 was viewed shunting the fourgon onto the remaining stub of the abandoned line to Le Cheylard at Lamastre, whilst running round the carriages on 15th August 2006. (P.Barnes)

4.31. A panoramic view of Lamastre station was recorded in June 1994. Among the sundry machinery visible are the Pétolat 4w loco-tractor no.PE-5, Billard A-80-D railcar no.314, one of the R-210 trailer cars and RM parcels van no.20. In the distance, Mallet no.404 has been coupled to its carriages prior to the late afternoon return service to Tournon. (J.Marsh)

4.32. SACM Mallet no.413 was recorded making a rousing departure from Lamastre with a train bound for Tournon during September 1992. Note that only the drain cocks of the rear high pressure cylinders are open. (J.F.Organ)

4.33. Shortly after leaving Lamastre, the line runs alongside the road before beginning the descent towards Monteil. No.413 was captured on the roadside section whilst hauling an afternoon train to Tournon during August 1994. (J.F.Organ)

4.34. During the course of the return journey to Tournon, a short ascent is encountered at Le Plat. No.413 was pictured at this location in September 1992, with a fourgon and two Swiss carriages immediately behind the locomotive. (J.F.Organ)

4.35. 0-6-6-0T Mallet no.403 passes 0-4-4-0T Mallet no.104 at Colombier-le-Vieux. No.403 was hauling the afternoon service train whilst no.104 was returning to Tournon with a charter mixed train on 12th October 2003. (F.Mottet)

4.36. A classic view of the Doux Gorge features Mallet no.404 hauling a colourful array of carriages, as the train threads its way down the gorge en-route to Tournon during the summer of 1982. (F.Collardeau/CFV coll.)

4.37. No.413 was viewed lower down the Doux Gorge near Clauzel as it hauled an assortment of Breton and Swiss carriages towards Tournon in 1989. (J.Dieu/CFV coll.)

4.38. No.403 was photographed on the final descent at the approach to Douce Plage on 3rd September 1996. This location, 5km from Tournon, is one of the most accessible viewing points on the CFV. (Mrs B.Organ)

4.39. The slender arch of the "Grand Pont" at Douce Plage is visible behind the pall of smoke as no.413 and its train drift alongside the river Doux in September 1998. (J.F.Organ)

4.40. No.403 draws into Tournon along the dual gauge SNCF track with a return train from Lamastre. This scene was recorded in 1978 before the overhead electrification was erected on the standard gauge route. (F.Collardeau/CFV coll.)

4.41. The same location 21 years later as Billard A-150-D no.213 and two trailer cars, plus A-80-D no. 314 attached to the rear of the ensemble, arrive from Lamastre during the morning of 18th July 1999. (J.F.Organ)

4.42. Billard A-80-D no.314 arrives at Tournon station during an uncharacteristic late fall of snow on 17th April 2005. (F.Mottet)

Locomotives, Railcars and Rolling Stock of the CFV

When the CFTM assumed control of the line in 1969, they were in a position to inherit the last remaining locomotives and five railcars plus most of the surviving passenger carriages and many freight vehicles. Much of this valuable equipment had been stored out of use for a number of years, however it provided the new organisation with a sound base on which to develop its future operation.

The five surviving Mallets were the major acquisitions. These included SLM locomotives nos 401, 403 and 404 and SACM nos 413 and 414. Of these nos 403 and 404 were in working order and were pressed into service immediately. No.401 has spent the last 38 years stored at Tournon, where it has been used as a source of spare parts. The two later locomotives, nos 413 and 414 both received major overhauls elsewhere, no.414 returning to service in 1972, whilst no.413 received a more protracted restoration which was completed in 1986. No.403 has been classified as a Monument Historique, which will certainly safeguard its future.

In addition to the steam locomotives, loco-tractors X and Y were transferred to the CFTM, along with the small Pétolet machine no.PE-5. The two loco-tractors have both been an invaluable asset to the railway, being used on a variety of tasks ranging from track maintenance work to hauling the occasional passenger train.

Following the closure of the CFD Vivarais, five railcars remained at Le Cheylard, the remainder having been transferred to Provence. These were De Dion ND no.207, Billard Type A-150-D nos 213 and 214 and Type A-80-D nos 314 and 316. The De Dion has remained in store at Lamastre since 1969 whilst the four Billards have seen regular continuous service. No.213 has received Monument Historique status, whilst no.316 spent many years in service for the permanent way department. This vehicle is now stored at Lamastre awaiting overhaul, having been relieved of its permanent way duties by a new service vehicle adapted from a standard gauge Billard railcar. In addition to the railcars, three of the R-210 trailer cars, nos 3,11 and 22 plus RM parcels van no.20, were also transferred to the CFTM. Seven railcars were also stored at Dunières and St.Agrève after 1968, these were ultimately to be acquired by the fledgling CFR operation.

Due to the fact that for many years, the majority of the passenger services were handled by railcars, only eight carriages remained at Le Cheylard in 1968. Of these, four Lorraine-Dietrich bogie carriages, nos 1609, 1658, 1661 and 1662, were acquired. The other Lorraine-Dietrich vehicle, no.1659, was still at Dunières and was destined to become part of the CFR / VFV stock. Three "Henhouses", nos 1751, 1801 and 1802 were also transferred to the CFTM, along with the Inspection Saloon no.1005. Four Fourgons and a large assortment of freight vehicles were also acquired. All these items of rolling stock have been classified as Monument Historique.

In order to supplement the two working locomotives, additional motive power was also provided by courtesy of FACS during the 1970s. These included no.31, a 1909 Pinguely 0-6-0T "Bi-Cabine" from the Tramways Quest-Dauphiné, a conventional 1905 Pinguely 0-6-0T (no.103) from Morbihan and two 1923 Corpet-Louvet 0-8-0Ts (nos 22 and 24) from an industrial line at Troyes. Of these additional locomotives, only nos 31 and 24 were suitable for use. No.103 was ultimately placed on a plinth near the river at Tournon, whilst no.22 spent a number of years on a plinth at the unlikely location of a motorway service station near Lyon. The unique "Bi-Cabine" no.31 has also gained the status of Monument Historique. In addition, FACS loaned their former Réseau Breton Fives-Lille 4 6-0T no. E-327 for a decade, until it was transferred to Provence in 1979. In 1971, a Blanc-Misseron 0-4-4-0T Mallet of 1906, no.104, from the PO Corrèze was delivered to Tournon. This locomotive had been acquired by a museum in the USA and was stored at Tournon until shipping could be arranged. During the course of these arrangements being made, the museum closed and no.104 was destined to remain in the care of the CFV. Having spent a number of years on display at Lamastre, this useful machine was officially donated to the CFTM in 1995 and restored to working order.

In addition to these locomotives, a total of 29 carriages were acquired from many sources throughout France and Switzerland. Notable items were eleven wooden bodied bogie carriages from the Réseau Breton, three from Provence plus three additional shorter bogie vehicles from Corrèze, which had originally worked on the Tramway de la Sarthe. As a consequence, this trio of carriages has become known as "The Sarthe Bogies". The Swiss carriages include 12 vehicles from lines that had been in the process of modernisation schemes, the majority from the various systems in the Lausanne and Montreux areas.

Other items of equipment that have arrived at Tournon include two interesting diesel powered machines. A Brissonneau et Lotz type ZM/ZR two-car Autorail was acquired from Spain in 1983. This powerful unit, powered by twin Berliet 150hp engines, was originally supplied to the CF Provence system in 1935. It was sold to the Santander-Bilbao line in 1951, where it worked until 1982. Since its acquisition for use on the CFV, it has been the subject of a protracted restoration project. The other more recent addition to the CFV stock also came from Provence. This is one of the CFD built B-B Diesel Hydraulics, no.402, which was originally delivered to the PO Corrèze in 1962. This of course is an identical "sister" of no.040-003, which was based at Le Cheylard between 1963 and 1968. Following its arrival in 2004, no.402 was to be the subject of another long-term restoration.

4.43.   SLM Mallet no.403 was viewed alongside the water tower at Tournon in readiness for hauling a train to Lamastre on 24th May 1998. (D.Trevor Rowe)

4.44.   Sister locomotive no.404 was recorded alongside the coal stage at Lamastre, prior to hauling an afternoon train back to Tournon in June 1994. (J.Marsh)

4.45. Fresh from a major overhaul, SACM Mallet no.414 is seen moving away from the water tower at Tournon depot before hauling a works train to Lamastre on 9th April 2004. (F.Mottet)

4.46. Former POC Corrèze Blanc-Misseron 0-4-4-0T Mallet no.104 was seen outside Tournon locoshed awaiting its next turn of duty during September 1998. (J.F.Organ)

4.47. Corpet-Louvet 0-8-0T no.24 was recorded at Boucieu-le-Roi, having hauled a charter freight train from Tournon on 23rd July 1994. This former industrial locomotive was for many years confined to the yard at Tournon, prior to the SNCF giving permission for it to traverse the dual gauge section. (F.Collardeau)

4.48. The unique Pinguely "Bi-Cabine" 0-6-0T was photographed being prepared for service at Tournon on 19th July 1999. The locomotive was scheduled to haul an afternoon train to Lamastre later that day. The cab at the forward end of the locomotive no longer contains any driving controls. (J.F.Organ)

4.49. *Of similar design, but with a conventional single cab, Pinguely 0-6-0T no.103 has been exhibited on a short length of track alongside the river at Tournon since 1986. It was viewed on 9th September 2006, shortly after receiving a re-paint. There were no plans to restore this locomotive to service. (J.F.Organ)*

4.50. *Following its return to service, the former POC Mallet no.104 was photographed at Douce Plage whilst on a test run on 13th September 1996. Note that loco-tractor "Y" is attached to the rear of the assembly – just in case! (F.Collardeau)*

4.51. Pinguely no.31 was recorded hauling a ballast train at Boucieu-le-Roi on 26th April 2005. Although these trains are normally hauled by one of the diesel locomotives, the steam locomotives are often pressed into service if the need arises. (F.Mottet)

4.52. An assorted line up of diesel powered machinery was recorded at Lamastre on 6th September 2006. Loco-tractor "X" was stabled in front of the Billard Draisine no.3 and the Pétolat no.PE-5. (J.F.Organ)

4.53. Photo-charter trains are a regular occurrence throughout the season on the CFV. Mallet no.104 drifts down towards Boucieu-le-Roi with a mixed train from Lamastre to Tournon on 12th October 2003. (F.Mottet).

4.54. Film and television contracts also provide lucrative additional revenue. During 2000, no.413 was re-painted in its original black livery in order to "star" in a film set during World War II. The film crew and some of the cast are seen alongside the locomotive at Boucieu-le-Roi on 1st October 2000. (F.Mottet)

4.55. No.413 retained its black livery until it was withdrawn for overhaul in 2002. The Mallet was recorded along with Billard no.214 at Lamastre on 9th September 2001. It is quite possible that the locomotive will retain the historic livery when it returns to service. (F.Mottet)

4.56. The Pinguely "Bi-Cabine" 0-6-0T is regularly used for driver experience courses, held between Boucieu-le-Roi and Colombier-le-Vieux. Following a week based at Boucieu for a series of courses, no.31 was double headed by no.414 as they hauled the empty stock of a charter mixed train down the upper reaches of the Doux Gorge near Colombier on 8th September 2006. (J.F.Organ)

PART 5 - VOIES FERREÉS DU VELAY

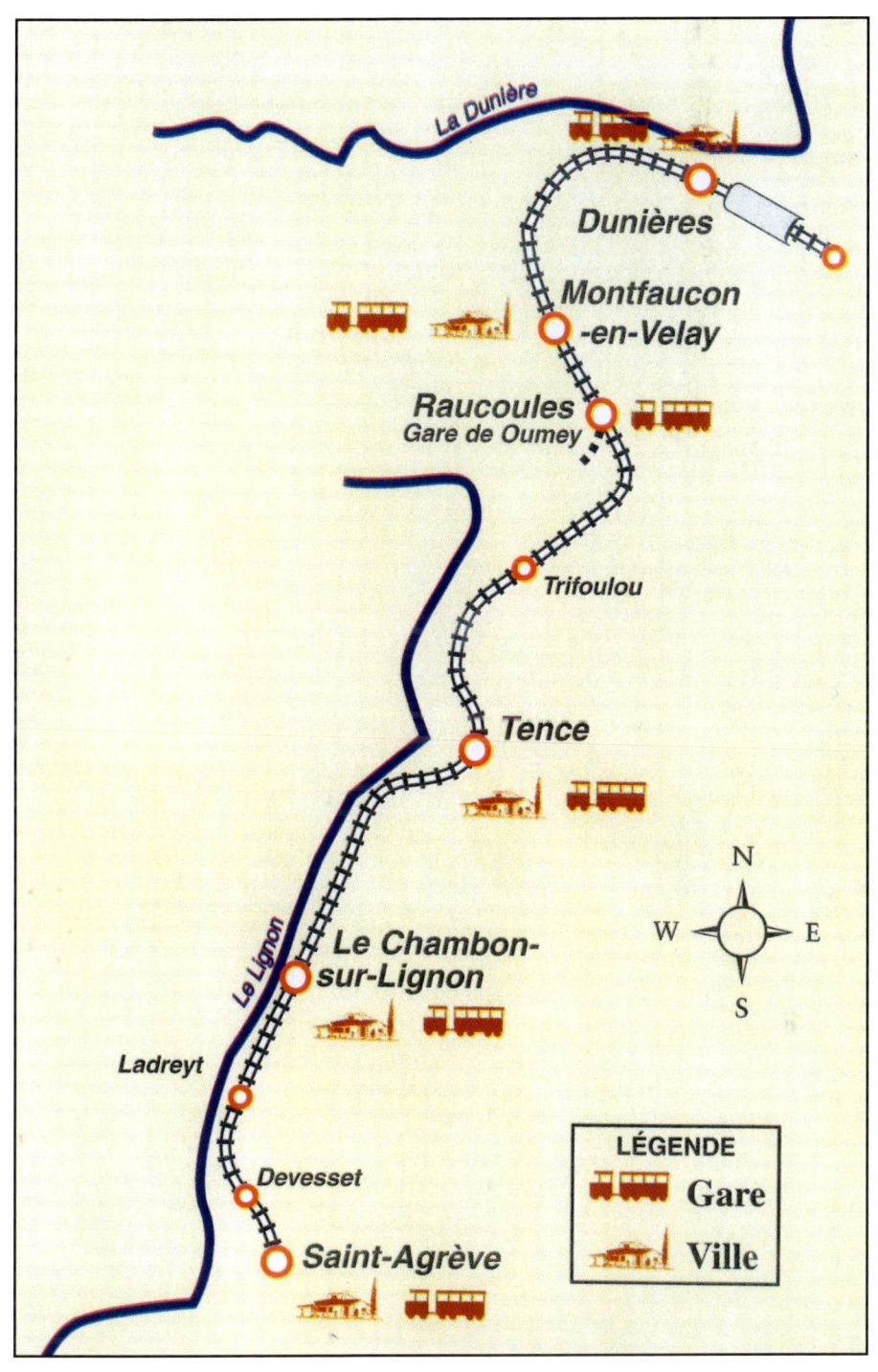

The early history of this preservation scheme in the Haute-Loire section of the Vivarais system was beset with many problems. In 1970, an organisation known as Les Chemins de Fer Régionaux (CFR) was granted authority to operate a tourist train service on the 36km (23 miles) line between Dunières and St.Agrève. At that time, this was the longest tourist railway in Europe. Although situated in a delightful area of rural landscapes, whilst also serving five small towns, it lacked the dramatic scenic attractions of the CFV route. However its major drawback was the accessibility to the major routes of the Rhône Valley, which was less convenient than that afforded to the Tournon based operation. Despite these problems, the CFR valiantly operated a service between 1970 and 1987, by which time the CFD lease had expired. Very few trains ran over the entire route, the majority worked between Dunières and Tence. A lesser number were operated between Tence and St.Agrève, notably during the months of high summer. Sadly, passenger numbers were not great enough to provide sufficient finance to purchase the line from CFD, nor to implement the many restoration projects that were required.

When the CFR took control of the line in 1970, they inherited the railcars that remained in store at Dunières. These included Billard A-150-D-2 articulated railcar no.222, Billard A-80-D single railcars nos 313 and 315, plus trailer car no.2 and De Dion type ND railcar no.206. In addition they received the remaining stock from Florac. These included loco-tractors nos 62 and 70, and three De Dion type ND railcars nos 201,202 and 204. With assistance from FACS, they were also donated two of the last items to remain in service on the recently closed PO Corrèze. These included a Billard A-150-D-1 railcar, no.X-153 and its trailer car no.R5. In addition, they received on long term loan from FACS a steam locomotive in the form of a POC Blanc-Misseron 0-4-4-0T Mallet no.101, dating from 1906, which is a sister of the Tournon based no.104.

No.101 has earned its place in history as being the last steam locomotive to operate on a French State owned narrow gauge line. Although in a well-worn condition when it arrived from Tulle in 1970, it was immediately pressed into service hauling the occasional steam hauled train. However the majority of the services were operated with the four railcars in working order, nos 204, 222, 313 and X-153. Rolling stock for the steam hauled trains consisted of one bogie carriage of Vivarais origin, Lorraine-Dietrich no.1659, plus some additional vehicles obtained from Brittany, Switzerland and Germany.

With an eye to the future, the principal director of the CFR, Gérard Prévôt, purchased one of the superb Piguet 0-6-6-0T Mallets that were built for use on the Réseau Breton in 1914. Although officially too heavy for the Vivarais track, it was hoped that by the time no.E-417 was restored, this situation could have been remedied. Also from the Breton line, one of the Decauville DXW railcars was acquired. No.X-232 was one of three constructed in 1940 for export to Indo-China. Due to the escalation of World War II, they remained in France until 1951 when they were sold to the SNCF for use in Brittany. With its twin Saurer 150hp power units, this impressive machine should have been an ideal vehicle for use on the CFR line. Sadly it was to remain in store at Tence. Another diesel locomotive added to the collection at this time was a further CFD loco-tractor. No 52 was acquired from Provence, although it had been constructed in 1948 for use on the CF du Tarn, where it was their no.LT2. This machine was in store at Raucoules-Brossettes awaiting a major overhaul.

During 1972, no.101 had to be withdrawn from service with boiler problems and was retired to the loco-shed at Tence, where it awaited a major overhaul when time and finance was available. With both Mallets unavailable, Gérard Prévôt purchased two small steam locomotives from what was then still East Germany. These were a 1903 built Henschel 0-6-0T, no.99 5611, from the Franzburger Kreisbahnen and a 1925 Borsig 0-4-0T, no.99 5001, that had previously been employed as a works shunter at Wernigerode Westerntor Works on the Harz system. The Henschel was almost immediately pressed into service on the occasional steam hauled services, its small size requiring it to receive banking assistance from one of the loco-tractors for the steep 1 in 33 ascent between Dunières and Montfaucon.

As explained, the CFD lease expired in 1985 and the CFR were not in a position to purchase the line. Sadly, the CFR operation ceased at the end of the 1987 season and nature rapidly began to reclaim the track. The two German locomotives and, ultimately, the Breton Mallet were removed to their owner's home at Valence. The railcars and rolling stock were left to deteriorate in the elements, apart from the vehicles fortunate enough to be housed undercover. The latter included the FACS owned POC Mallet, no.101, the last surviving Billard articulated railcar no.222, Billards nos 313 and X-153 and De Dion no.204.

5.1. The first steam locomotive to operate on the CFR was the former POC Corrèze 0-4-4-0T Mallet no.101, which is owned by FACS. The locomotive was recorded at Argentat, shortly before the POC closed on 1st June 1970, just prior to it being transferred to Dunières. (Colour-Rail)

5.2. No.101 was viewed at St.Agrève with a short train consisting of former Réseau Breton and Mittelbadische Eisenbahnen (MEG) carriages during November 1972, shortly before the locomotive was withdrawn from service. (H. Tenoux)

5.3. Following the withdrawal of no.101, the occasional steam worked services on the CFR were hauled by a Henschel 0-6-0T, which formerly worked at the Franzburger Kreisbahnen on the Baltic Coast of Germany. No.99 5611 was recorded at Tence with a train from Dunières in August 1977. (J.F.Organ coll.)

5.4. De Dion Bouton type ND railcar no.204 and former Breton/Corrèze Billard type A-150-D-1 railcar no.X-153 were photographed at Tence, en-route from Dunières to St.Agrève, in July 1981. (H.Tenoux)

5.5. *Former Réseau Breton Piguet 0-6-6-0T Mallet no. E-417 and Tarn / Provence CFD loco-tractor no.52 were viewed at Raucoules-Brossettes, awaiting restoration, in June 1994. The Mallet was shortly destined to be removed to its owners home near Valence, whilst no.52 remained in store at the same location. (J.Marsh)*

In 1992 a new organisation was formed with the intention of saving the dormant railway. Voies Ferrées du Velay (VFV) began the task of clearing the undergrowth that was rapidly taking control of the track, whilst some of the locomotives and rolling stock were returned to service. During the period of closure, the extensive metre gauge exchange sidings at Dunières had disappeared under a new road scheme, whilst a number of level crossings had also been "lost" as a result of road resurfacing work. However, despite these obstacles, a limited service was offered between Dunières Ville and Montfaucon during 1993. This stretch of line 6km(4 miles) in length, which incorporates a gradient of 1in33, was operated by loco-tractors nos 62 or 70 and two carriages of Swiss and German origin. By 1994, the track between Montfaucon and Tence had been cleared allowing a journey of 17km (11 miles) along the undulating and rural route. Happily, these initial operations were successful enough to encourage the VFV to restore the remainder of the route, in addition to returning to service other items of stock they had inherited.

Billard A-150-D-2 articulated railcar no.222 re-entered service late in 1996 and was the first vehicle to pass through the restored tunnel between Dunières SNCF and Dunières Ville stations. During 1997, this splendid machine was joined by the Billard A-80-D railcar no.313, both railcars working alongside the two former Lozère loco-tractors. Meanwhile, POC Mallet no.101 remained in the locoshed at Tence awaiting a major overhaul. During the final years of the 1990s, the track over the high plateau and watershed between Tence and St.Agrève was progressively restored, whilst the stations at Tence, Le Chambon-sur-Lignon and St.Agrève were also restored to their former glory. The entire 36km (23 miles) route was finally operational for the 2000 season. The operation was basically divided into two sections with the diesel locomotives normally hauling trains between Dunières and Tence or Le Chambon, whilst the two railcars were based at St.Agrève for use on the upper section of the line. On summer Saturdays, a railcar service has been operating over the entire route between St.Agrève and Dunières.

During the last decade, a close working relationship has been developed between the VFV and CFV. This resulted in the transfer of Mallet no.403 to St.Agrève during September 2002 in order for it to be the major attraction at the centenary celebrations of the Haute-Loire section of the Vivarais network. No.403 worked over the entire route between St.Agrève and Dunières, an event that attracted a great deal of interest.

In 2004, the FACS owned Corpet-Louvet 0-8-0T, no.22, was removed from the plinth at Lyon it had occupied for 30 years and delivered to Tence for restoration. Currently both nos 101 and 22 are in course of major overhauls in a workshop at Tence, a short distance from the railway. Negotiations have taken place between the CFV and VFV with a view to transferring on long term loan the pioneer SLM Mallet, no. 401, to Tence after the restoration of one of the two FACS locomotives has been completed. Having stood in a partially dismantled state at Tournon since 1969, being used as a source of spare parts, it would be very fitting for this historic locomotive to be rebuilt and used on the VFV. No. 401 was based at St. Agrève for the majority of its active life.

The Route - Dunières to St. Agrève

The most northerly station on the Réseau du Vivarais was situated at Dunières Ville, although the actual terminus was at Dunières SNCF (formerly PLM). The two stations were separated by a short tunnel, which passed under the lower part of the hillside town. In addition to the former terminal station, situated alongside the now closed SNCF station and the site of the once extensive transhipment sidings, Dunières has a small depot consisting of a single road engine shed, railcar shed, turntable, water-tower and coal stage. The engine shed is currently in use for rolling stock restoration, whilst the railcar shed is in use for its original purpose.

Due to its more central position, the majority of trains now depart from Dunières Ville. Almost immediately after leaving the station, there begins the steep climb on a 1 in 33 gradient for most of the 6km (4 miles) to Montfaucon. The line then adopts a very twisty and undulating route for 3km (2 miles) to the former junction at Raucoules-Brossettes. Here the short stump of the long closed line to La Voûte sur Loire branches off to the right. This became a siding used to store some of the derelict stock, hopefully awaiting restoration in the future. More derelict items were stored in the sidings near the station and loco-shed, where two fuel pumps are located for replenishing the fuel tanks of the diesel powered machines.

The 7km(4.5 miles) between Raucoules-Brossettes and Tence is through a typically rural French landscape as the line twists and turns between the adjacent road and meadows. The station at Tence occupies an extensive site with numerous sidings plus a loco-shed and turntable at the southern end of the complex. Many items of stock are stored there, some awaiting restoration. As the major intermediate station, many of the VFV services terminate at Tence – operating either over the northern or southern section of the route.

From Tence, there follows an 8.5km (5 miles) climb mainly through woodland above the upper reaches of the Lignon Gorge. This is arguably the most scenic section of the route as it climbs towards the attractive town of Le Chambon sur Lignon, which has many alpine characteristics in its appearance. The final 9kms (6 miles) from Le Chambon to St.Agrève climbs onto the high plateau, culminating in the 1060m summit at the watershed of the Atlantic and Mediterranean. This is also the boundary between the Haute-Loire and Ardèche Dèpartements, where snow fences used to protect the line during the harsh winter months. Some superb views can be obtained from this elevated section of the route. A distant landmark is the distinctive conical mount of Gerbier de Joncs, from where the Loire makes its first appearance before its long circuitous journey to the Atlantic coast. The extensive station complex at St.Agrève is reached following a short 1 in 33 descent from the summit. The station building is situated opposite the two road locoshed, beyond which there used to be a level crossing leading to the now abandoned line descending through the Eyrieux Gorge to Le Cheylard. The two operational railcars are based at St.Agrève, the large depot being an ideal base for their storage and maintenance.

5.6. The first train to operate under VFV control was recorded arriving at Montfaucon on 22nd August 1993, hauled by former CFD Lozère loco-tractor no.62. During the first season of the VFV operation, trains only ran on the 4km (3 miles) section between Dunières Ville and Montfaucon. (H.Tenoux)

5.7. No. 62 is soon to depart from Dunières Ville with a train bound for Le Chambon-sur-Lignon on 1st October 2006. This was the final regular operating day of the 2006 season. (F.Mottet)

5.8. Billard type A-80-D railcar no.313 ascends the upper part of the 1 in 33 climb between Dunières Ville and Montfaucon on 6th July 2002. The railcars are normally based at St.Agrève and usually only work to Dunières on Saturdays during the high season. (F.Mottet)

5.9. Loco-tractor no.62 pauses with its single Swiss carriage at Raucoules-Brossettes whilst en-route to Le Chambon-sur-Lignon on 1st October 2006. The original "bull-nose" radiator surround of no.62 was replaced with the flat design, now fitted, by the CFR during a major overhaul in the 1970s. (F.Mottet)

5.10. Nos 62 and 70 were recorded at Tence, prior to double heading a train to Dunières Ville on 28th August 1996. One of the semi-open carriages, constructed by the VFV on the frames of a former freight wagon, was marshalled next to no.62. (J.F.Organ)

5.11. CFD loco-tractor no.62 hauls a train through a delightful tree lined section of line, high above the Lignon Gorge. The train was en-route from Dunières Ville to Le Chambon-sur-Lignon on 10th September 2006. (J.F.Organ)

5.12. The same train enters Le Chambon, passing the level crossing a short distance from the station, on a bright Sunday morning in September 2006. *(Mrs.B.Organ)*

5.13. Another view of no.62 was recorded as it departed from Le Chambon-sur-Lignon en-route to Dunières on 1st October 2006. *(F.Mottet)*

5.14.   Billard railcars A-150-D-2 no.222 and A-80-D no.313 climb onto the plateau between Le Chambon and St.Agrève on 6th July 2002. This exposed section of the Vivarais route was notorious for heavy snow during the winter months in the CFD era, snow fences originally protected the line in many places. (F.Mottet)

5.15.   Articulated Billard A-150-D-2 railcar no.222 was viewed at the superbly restored station at St.Agrève, prior to departing with a special winter service to Dunières on 11th December 2004. (F.Mottet)

5.16.   Adorned with the Flèche des Cévennes insignia of the late 1940s, no.222 was recorded shortly after departing from St.Agrève. The location is near the summit of the line, which also marks the boundary between the Ardèche and Haute-Loire, and forms the watershed between the Mediterranean and Atlantic. (F.Mottet)

5.17.   Loco-tractor no.70 was photographed entering Tence with a short freight train on 6th July 2002. De Dion type NE railcar trailer no.1 is attached to the rear of the assembly. (F.Mottet)

Locomotives, Railcars and Rolling Stock of the VFV

When the VFV took possession of the railway and equipment in 1992, the only useable items were the two Lozère loco-tractors and three carriages. The situation has recently improved greatly, although many items are still in store awaiting restoration.

No.101, the POC 0-4-4-0T Mallet, was the sole steam locomotive remaining following the demise of the CFR. The Mallet, which is still owned by FACS, had remained in the shed at Tence since 1972. An initial evaluation was carried out at Tence, prior to the locomotive being transferred to a nearby workshop for a comprehensive rebuild. In 2004 it was joined by another FACS owned machine. Corpet-Louvet 0-8-0T no.22 had for many years occupied a plinth at a motorway service area near Lyon, where it had acted as a "three dimensional" advertisement for the CFV. No.22 has an interesting history, having been sent to Jersey in 1943 for use on construction lines for the German fortifications. It is possibly the only locomotive to have been driven by German servicemen on British territory.

The two former Lozère loco-tractors nos 62 and 70 have handled the majority of the traffic since 1993, whilst the former Tarn/Provence machine no.52 is currently in store at Raucoules-Brossettes awaiting restoration. The diesel locomotives have proved to be an invaluable asset in maintaining the service during the ensuing years.

The Billard A-150-D-2 articulated railcar no.222 was returned to service for the 1997 season, to be joined a short time later by A-80-D unit no.313. These are based at St.Agrève from where they operate principally to Tence, apart from the summer Saturday excursions to Dunières. De Dion ND railcar no.204 and Billard A-150-D-1 no.X-153 are both stored in the railcar shed at Dunières, along with De Dion NE trailer car no.1, awaiting a return to service. Also stored in the yard at Dunières is Billard A-80-D no.315 in poor condition.

De Dion ND railcars nos 201 and 206 are stored in a derelict condition at Raucoules-Brossettes, whilst the former Réseau Breton Decauville DXW no.X-232 is stored in the yard at Tence. Also derelict at Raucoules are Billard trailer cars nos 2 and R5, whilst at Tence the Billard RM and CFD parcels vans nos 30 and 40 are in store.

Passenger rolling stock in service includes three Réseau Breton bogie carriages, and two vehicles from Switzerland and Germany. In addition, two semi-open carriages have been constructed on the frames of former freight wagons. Stored in the shed at Tence is the only carriage of Vivarais origin, Lorraine-Dietrich bogie no.1659, along with two former Rhätische Bahn 4 wheeled carriages. Another Breton bogie carriage is currently under restoration in the loco-shed at Dunières. These will undoubtedly be required when steam hauled trains become a regular feature of the VFV operation, along with two former Vivarais fourgons that are currently in store at Tence.

5.18. The weekend of 27th-29th September 2002 was a momentous occasion for the VFV. In order to celebrate the centenary of the Dunières to St.Agrève section of the Réseau Vivarais and also the 10th anniversary of the VFV, SLM Mallet no.403 was transferred from Tournon for the duration of the celebrations. No.403 was photographed alongside A-150-D-2 railcar no.222 at St.Agrève depot on 28th September. (F.Mottet)

5.19. On the previous day, the Mallet was recorded revisiting Dunières depot for the first time since 1968. No.403 was a regular locomotive on this section of the route during the latter years of the CFD era. (F.Mottet)

5.20.   No.403 and its carriages provided a wonderful spectacle as the train ascended the 1 in 33 climb between Dunières Ville and Montfaucon on 29th September 2002. (F.Mottet)

5.21.   Nearing the end of the same journey, the Mallet climbs from Le Chambon-sur-Lignon towards the high plateau, whilst a Traction Avant Citroen waits at a level crossing. (F.Mottet)

5.22. *No.403 returns to its former home at St.Agrève, having hauled a train from Dunières on 27th September 2002. With the possible restoration of sister locomotive no.401 at Tence, similar scenes will hopefully become a regular occurrence in the future activities of the VFV. (L.Manoha/F.Mottet coll.)*

5.23. *The FACS owned Corpet-Louvet 0-8-0T no.22, which had spent many years on a plinth near Lyon, was eventually transported to Tence for restoration to working condition. The locomotive was recorded at Bourg-Argental, en-route to Tence on 29th September 2004. (F.Mottet)*

Part 6 - THE 60cm GAUGE CONNECTION

As previously mentioned, the CFTM had its origins during the late1950s when a group of Lyon based enthusiasts began to gather together a collection of 60cm gauge locomotives from industrial and agricultural lines throughout France. These were mainly drawn from the sugar beet lines such as Pithiviers and Maizy.

Meyzieu

In order to restore and operate their acquisitions, the Chemin de Fer Touristique du Meyzieu was established at Mezieu in the eastern outskirts of Lyon. Here a short, mainly roadside, tramway was laid whilst some basic rolling stock was constructed from adapted freight wagons. Among the seven locomotives collected were two Decauvilles, a 0-4-0T (no.1) and a 0-6-0T (no.3) of 1912 and 1922 vintage respectively. These were joined by a 1910 Couillet 0-6-0T (no.2) and a 1938 La Meuse 2-6-0T (no.8), both from Maizy. One of the ubiquitous "Feldbahn" 0-8-0Ts (no.743) was also acquired, this example being a 1917 Krauss version. From Pithiviers an O&K 0-4-4-0T Mallet (no.22-5) of 1905 and one of the impressive 1944 Franco-Belge Type KDL 0-8-0Ts (no.4-13) completed the collection.

The CFTM operated a weekend service on the short line during the 1960s. However, by 1970 the site was required for building development, as the suburbs of Lyon began to encroach upon the countryside. This period also coincided with the early stage of the CFTM involvement with operating the CFV, which restricted their activities with the smaller gauge railway. As a consequence, the stock was stored away at a secure location near Lyon until a new site for the railway could be located.

Montalieu

It was to be 1988 before a suitable location for the railway could be found. This was at Montalieu, about 65km (40miles) east of Lyon on the banks of the Rhône. The track was relaid as an attractive riverside tramway, whilst passenger comfort was improved following the purchase of five carriages from the tramways at Neufchatel and Valenciennes. Now renamed Chemin de Fer du Haute-Rhône, the re-established line continued to be operated by the CFTM until 2004, when it was transferred to a new operator under the leadership of Monsieur J.Hoos. Following their long period of storage, the locomotives required overhauls prior to re-entering service. One was restored by the CFVO at Bligny, whilst this organisation has subsequently purchased two of the locomotives. The delightful CFHR at Montalieu operated a Sunday service in 2007 between May and October, plus a Saturday service during July and August. Motive power was provided by either the 0-6-0T Decauville or the Krauss "Feldbahn", with the O&K Mallet as reserve.

Chemin de Fer de la Vallée de l'Ouche (CFVO)

This 60cm gauge railway began operation in 1978, being built on the track-bed of a standard gauge line originally constructed in 1837 as a colliery railway. Subsequently adapted as a conventional passenger and freight railway, the standard gauge line was closed by SNCF in 1968. The CFVO was conceived in conjunction with the local council and its headquarters were established at the station at Bligny, a typically French village a short distance to the north of Beaune.

The President of the CFVO, Jean Claude Laboureau, has become well known as a fireman on the Festiniog Railway during his twice-annual visits to North Wales. When operation of the 7km (4.5 miles) 60cm gauge line commenced in 1978, the only locomotive was a 1947 Decauville 0-4-0TT, based on a Henschel design. In order to provide additional motive power, the Krauss "Feldbahn" 0-8-0T was loaned from the former Meyzieu stock and restored to working order. This locomotive paid a visit to Porthmadog in 1995, in order to participate in the FR Gala event of that year.

In 1999 the 0-6-0T Couillet was purchased from the CFTM and overhauled to an excellent condition. The Krauss "Feldbahn" was subsequently returned to Montalieu in 2002, since when it has been in regular service. In return, the CFVO received the Franco-Belge KDL 0-8-0T and the La Meuse 2-6-0T, both of which required major overhauls. The Belgian built 2-6-0T had arrived via Pithiviers, where the overhaul was begun, sister locomotive from Maizy (no.9) being in regular service on that line.

This splendid railway operates on Sundays between May and September, plus a daily service during July and August. Whilst not originally a narrow gauge railway, the CFVO provides an atmospheric reminder of the minor lines of France, as it passes through the delightful Burgundy countryside. Although it has never been connected with the CFTM and Vivarais organisation, it has been included in this section due to its close working arrangements with the Montalieu operation.

6.1.   Decauville "Type Progrès" 0-6-0T, no.3, stands in a passing loop at Meyzieu, whilst the Couillet 0-6-0T waits behind, on 7th May 1966. (D. Trevor Rowe)

6.2.   The former Pithiviers O&K 0-4-4-0T Mallet accelerates away from Meyzieu on the same occasion. The location of this short railway has now been swallowed up by extensive developments of the Lyon suburbs. (D.Trevor Rowe)

6.3.   A more detailed view of the German built 60cm gauge Mallet, a number of which worked in France after WWI. Still carrying its Pithiviers number 22-5, the locomotive was recorded at the far terminus of the Meyzieu line on 7th May 1966. (D.Trevor Rowe)

6.4. Forty years later, the Decauville 0-6-0T was photographed at the outer terminus of the CF Haute Rhône at Sault-Brenag, having hauled a train of former Neufchatel and Valenciennes tramway carriages from Montalieu during the summer of 2006. (J.Arrivetz)

6.5. The Krauss "Feldbahn" 0-8-0T no.743 was recorded during its tenure at the Chemin de Fer de la Vallée de l'Ouche (CFVO). The former German military locomotive was viewed entering the station at Bligny during July 2002, whilst the Couillet 0-6-0T can be seen in the distance. (J.C.Laboureau)

6.6. The former Maizy sugar refinery Couillet 0-6-0T, which was purchased from the CFTM in 1999, was photographed outside the depot at Bligny on 9th January 2007. As can be seen from this view, its new owners have restored the locomotive to a high standard. (J.C.Laboureau)

6.7. Awaiting a comprehensive overhaul, former Pithiviers Franco-Belge type KDL 0-8-0T no.4-13 was recorded at Bligny on 9th January 2007. Although this locomotive was purchased by the CFTM for the Meyzieu operation in 1967, it has always remained in store. (J.C.Laboureau)

Part 7 - CFV and VFV LOCOMOTIVES, RAILCARS AND CARRIAGES

Both organisations, involved in operating the two surviving sections of the Vivarais system, have between them saved a huge amount of the motive power and rolling stock from the original line. In addition, they have acquired many items from other French metre gauge lines, which have resulted in a wonderfully representative collection of stock from these sadly missed railways.

No.	Type	Constructor	Origin	Status 2007
STEAM LOCOMOTIVES				
401	0-6-6-0T	SLM (1902)	Vivarais	CFV (stored)
403	0-6-6-0T	SLM (1903)	Vivarais	CFV (active)
404	0-6-6-0T	SLM (1903)	Vivarais	CFV (overhaul)
413	0-6-6-0T	SACM (1932)	Vivarais	CFV (overhaul)
414	0-6-6-0T	SACM (1932)	Vivarais	CFV (active)
101	0-4-4-0T	Blanc-Misseron (1906)	Corrèze	VFV (overhaul)
104	0-4-4-0T	Blanc-Misseron (1906)	Corrèze	CFV (active)
22	0-8-0T	Corpet-Louvet (1923)	Frot-Troyes	VFV (overhaul)
24	0-8-0T	Corpet-Louvet (1923)	Frot-Troyes	CFV (active)
31	0-6-0T	Pinguely (1909)	Quest du Dauphiné	CFV (active).
103	0-6-0T	Pinguely (1905)	Morbihan	CFV (plinthed).
DIESEL LOCOMOTIVES				
X	0-6-0	CFD Vivarais (1948)	Vivarais	CFV (active)
Y	0-6-0	CFD Vivarais (1948)	Vivarais	CFV (active)
62	0-6-0	CFD Montmirail (1946)	Lozère	VFV (active)
70	0-6-0	CFD Montmirail (1948)	Lozère	VFV (active)
52	0-6-0	CFD Montmirail (1948)	Tarn / Provence	VFV (stored)
Pe-5	4w	Pétolat (1930)	Vivarais	CFV (stored)
402	B-B DH	CFD Montmirail (1962)	Corrèze / Provence	CFV (stored)

RAILCARS

201	ND	De Dion Bouton (1935)	Lozère	VFV (stored)
204	ND	De Dion Bouton (1935)	Vivarais / Lozère	VFV (stored)
206	ND	De Dion Bouton (1935)	Vivarais	VFV (stored)
207	ND	De Dion Bouton (1935)	Vivarais	CFV (stored)
213	A-150-D	Billard (1938)	Vivarais	CFV (active)
214	A-150-D	Billard (1940)	Vivarais	CFV (active)
222	A-150-D-2	Billard (1939)	Vivarais	VFV (active)
313	A-80-D	Billard (1937)	Charentes / Vivarais	VFV (active)
314	A-80-D	Billard (1937)	Charentes / Vivarais	CFV (active)
315	A-80-D	Billard (1938)	Charentes / Vivarais	VFV (stored)
316	A-80-D	Billard (1938)	Charentes / Vivarais	CFV (overhaul)
X-153	A-150-D-1	Billard (1937)	Breton / Corrèze	VFV (stored)
ZM 8 / ZR 4		Brissoneau et Lotz (1935)	Provence	CFV (stored)
X-232		Decauville (1940)	Breton	VFV (stored)

RAILCAR PASSENGER TRAILERS

1	NE	De Dion Bouton (1935)	Lozère	VFV (stored)
2	R-210	Billard (1938)	Vivarais	VFV (stored)
3	R-210	Billard (1938)	Vivarais	CFV (active)
11	R-210	Billard (1937)	Charentes / Vivarais	CFV (active)
22	R-210	Billard (1937)	Charentes / Vivarais	CFV (active)
R5	R-150	Billard (1937)	Breton / Corrèze	VFV (stored)

RAILCAR LUGGAGE TRAILERS

20	RM	Billard (1937)	Charentes / Vivarais	CFV (active)

30	RM	Billard (1937)	Charentes / Vivarais	VFV (stored)
40	CFD	CFD Vivarais (1967)	Vivarais	VFV (stored)
59	NF	De Dion Bouton (1935)	Vivarais / Lozère	VFV (stored)
60	NF	De Dion Bouton (1935)	Vivarais / Lozère	VFV (stored)

PASSENGER CARRIAGES

1005	4w Saloon	De Dietrich (1902)	Vivarais	CFV (active)
1427	Bogie(3rd)	De Dietrich (1902)	Vivarais	CFV (restoration)
1751	4w Comp.	De Dietrich (1904)	Vivarais	CFV (active)
1801	4w (3rd)	De Dietrich (1904)	Vivarais	CFV (active)
1802	4w (3rd)	De Dietrich (1904)	Vivarais	CFV (active)
1609	Bogie Comp.	Lorraine-Dietrich (1931)	Vivarais	CFV (active)
1658	Bogie (3rd)	Lorraine-Dietrich (1927)	Vivarais	CFV (active)
1659	Bogie (3rd)	Lorraine-Dietrich (1927)	Vivarais	VFV (stored)
1661	Bogie (3rd)	Lorraine-Dietrich (1927)	Vivarais	CFV (active)
1662	Bogie (3rd)	Lorraine-Dietrich (1927)	Vivarais	CFV (active)

In addition to the above carriages of Vivarais origin, both the CFV and VFV have preserved a large collection of "end balcony" vehicles from elsewhere in France, plus examples from Switzerland and Germany. A large number of freight vehicles have also been saved, including nine luggage vans (fourgons) of which six are of CFD Vivarais origin.

TRACK MAINTENANCE VEHICLES (DRAISINE)

1	4w	Campagne (1932)	Vivarais	CFV (active)
2	4w	Campagne (1932)	Charentes / Vivarais	CFV (stored)
3	Orig. A-75-D	Billard (1957)	SNCF (std gauge)	CFV (active)

MONTALIEU AND BLIGNY 60cm GAUGE STEAM LOCOMOTIVES

1	0-4-0T	Decauville (1912)	Courzieu	Montalieu (static)
3	0-6-0T	Decauville (1922)	Luzy	Montalieu (active)

22-5	0-4-4-0T	O&K	(1905)	Pithiviers	Montalieu (active)
743	0-8-0T	Krauss	(1917)	Chagny	Montalieu (active)
2	0-6-0T	Couillet	(1910)	Maizy	Bligny (active)
8	2-6-0T	La Meuse	(1938)	Maizy	Bligny (overhaul-for Montalieu)
1	0-4-0TT	Decauville	(1947)	Industrial	Bligny (active)
4-13	0-8-0T	Franco-Belge	(1944)	Pithiviers	Bligny (stored)

ENCORE

Although the Réseau du Vivarais closed in 1968, its legacy has not been forgotten thanks to the joint efforts of the CFV and VFV. With two contrasting sections of the Vivarais system still operating under the control of these two organisations, the future prospects for this railway that positively refused to die are most definitely assured.

Tournon is easily reached by rail. TGV services from Paris and Lille serve Valence, which can be reached from London in about six hours. A local train or a bus can be used for the final leg of the journey from Valence to Tournon. A bus service from Tournon serves St.Agrève, whilst Tence and Dunières can be reached by bus from St.Agrève or St.Etienne. For the serious photographers, a car is almost essential to find the majority of the more remote line-side locations!

Ffestiniog Travel, Harbour Station, Porthmadog, Gwynedd, LL49 9NF (Tel:- 01766 512400) often include the area in their European Holidays, whilst they can also assist in planning a "tailor made" itinerary to suit individual requirements.

Further information regarding the railways featured in this publication can be obtained from the following addresses:-

Chemin de Fer du Vivarais, Avenue de la Gare, 07300, Tournon, France.
Tel:- 04 75 08 20 30. Fax:- 04 75 07 01 77.

Voies Ferrées du Velay, 22 rue de la Croix, 43220, Dunières, France.
Tel / Fax:- 04 71 61 94 44.

For the 60cm gauge enthusiasts, the two smaller operations can be contacted at:-

Chemin de Fer du Haute-Rhône, c/o Office de Tourisme, 69440, Montalieu, France.
Tel:- 04 78 81 84 30. Fax:- 04 78 81 67 45.

Le Chemin de Fer Vallée de L'Ouche, 21360, Bligny-sur-Ouche, France.
Tel / Fax:- 03 80 20 17 92.

MP Middleton Press
EVOLVING THE ULTIMATE RAIL ENCYCLOPEDIA
Easebourne Lane, Midhurst, West Sussex.
GU29 9AZ Tel:01730 813169
www.middletonpress.co.uk email:info@middletonpress.co.uk
A-0 906520 B-1 873793 C-1 901706 D-1 904474
OOP Out of print at time of printing - Please check availability BROCHURE AVAILABLE SHOWING NEW TITLES

A
Abergavenny to Merthyr C 91 8
Abertillery and Ebbw Vale Lines D 84 5
Aldgate & Stepney Tramways B 70 1
Allhallows - Branch Line to A 62 8
Alton - Branch Lines to A 11 6
Andover to Southampton A 82 6
Ascot - Branch Lines around A 64 2
Ashburton - Branch Line to B 95 4
Ashford - Steam to Eurostar B 67 1
Ashford to Dover A 48 2
Austrian Narrow Gauge D 04 3
Avonmouth - BL around D 42 5
Aylesbury to Rugby D 91 3
B
Baker Street to Uxbridge D 90 6
Banbury to Birmingham D 27 2
Barking to Southend C 80 2
Barnet & Finchley Tramways B 93 0
Barry - Branch Lines around D 50 0
Basingstoke to Salisbury A 89 5
Bath Green Park to Bristol C 36 9
Bath to Evercreech Junction A 60 4
Bath Tramways B 86 2
Battle over Portsmouth 1940 A 29 1
Battle over Sussex 1940 A 79 6
Bedford to Wellingborough D 31 9
Betwixt Petersfield & Midhurst A 94 9
Bletchley to Cambridge D 94 4
Bletchley to Rugby E 07 9
Blitz over Sussex 1941-42 B 35 0
Bodmin - Branch Lines around B 83 1
Bognor at War 1939-45 B 59 6
Bombers over Sussex 1943-45 B 51 0
Bournemouth & Poole Trys B 47 3
Bournemouth to Evercreech Jn A 46 8
Bournemouth to Weymouth A 57 4
Bournemouth Trolleybuses C 10 9
Bradford Trolleybuses D 19 7
Brecon to Neath D 43 2
Brecon to Newport D 16 6
Brecon to Newtown E 06 2
Brickmaking in Sussex B 19 0
Brightons Tramways B 02 2 OOP
Brighton to Eastbourne A 16 1
Brighton to Worthing A 03 1
Brighton Trolleybuses D 34 0
Bristols Tramways B 57 2
Bristol to Taunton D 03 6
Bromley South to Rochester B 23 7
Bromsgrove to Birmingham D 87 6
Bromsgrove to Gloucester D 73 9
Brunel - A railtour of his achievements D 74 6
Bude - Branch Line to B 29 9
Burnham to Evercreech Jn A 68 0
Burton & Ashby Tramways C 51 2
C
Camberwell & West Norwood Tys B 22 0
Cambridge to Ely D 55 5
Canterbury - Branch Lines around B 58 9
Cardiff Trolleybuses D 64 7
Caterham & Tattenham Corner B 25 1
Changing Midhurst C 15 4
Chard and Yeovil - BLs around C 30 7
Charing Cross to Dartford A 75 8
Charing Cross to Orpington A 96 3
Cheddar - Branch Line to B 90 9
Cheltenham to Andover C 43 7
Cheltenham to Redditch D 81 4
Chesterfield Tramways D 37 1
Chesterfield Trolleybuses D 51 7
Chester Tramways E 04 8
Chichester to Portsmouth A 14 7
Clapham & Streatham Trys B 97 8
Clapham Junction - 50 yrs C 06 2 OOP
Clapham Junction to Beckenham Jn B 36 7
Clevedon & Portishead - BLs to D 18 0
Collectors Trains, Trolleys & Trams D 29 6
Colonel Stephens D62 3
Cornwall Narrow Gauge D 56 2
Cowdray & Easebourne D 96 8
Crawley to Littlehampton A 34 5
Cromer - Branch Lines around C 26 6
Croydons Tramways B 42 8
Croydons Trolleybuses B 73 2 OOP
Croydon to East Grinstead B 48 0
Crystal Palace (HL) & Catford Loop A 87 1
D
Darlington to Newcastle D 98 2
Darlington Trolleybuses D 33 3
Dartford to Sittingbourne B 34 3
Derby Tramways D 17 3
Derby Trolleybuses C 72 7
Derwent Valley - Branch Line to the D 06 7
Devon Narrow Gauge E 09 3
Didcot to Banbury D 02 9
Didcot to Swindon C 84 0
Didcot to Winchester C 13 0
Dorset & Somerset Narrow Gauge D 76 0
Douglas to Peel C 88 8
Douglas to Port Erin C 55 0
Douglas to Ramsey D 39 5
Dovers Tramways B 24 4
Dover to Ramsgate A 78 9
E
Ealing to Slough C 42 0
Eastbourne to Hastings A 27 7 OOP
East Cornwall Mineral Railways D 22 7
East Croydon to Three Bridges A 53 6
East Grinstead - Branch Lines to A 07 9
East Ham & West Ham Tramways B 52 7
East Kent Light Railway A 61 1 OOP
East London - Branch Lines of C 44 4
East London Line B 80 0
East Ridings Secret Resistance D 21 0
Edgware & Willesden Tramways C 18 5
Effingham Junction - BLs around A 74 1
Eltham & Woolwich Tramways B 74 9 OOP
Ely to Kings Lynn C 53 6
Ely to Norwich C 90 1
Embankment & Waterloo Tramways B 41 1
Enfield & Wood Green Trys C 03 1 OOP
Enfield Town & Palace Gates - BL to D 32 6
Epsom to Horsham A 30 7
Euston to Harrow & Wealdstone C 89 5
Exeter & Taunton Tramways B 32 9
Exeter to Barnstaple B 15 2
Exeter to Newton Abbot C 49 9
Exeter to Tavistock B 69 5
Exmouth - Branch Lines to B 00 8
F
Fairford - Branch Line to A 52 9
Falmouth, Helston & St. Ives - BL to C 74 1
Fareham to Salisbury A 67 3
Faversham to Dover B 05 3
Felixstowe & Aldeburgh - BL to D 20 3
Fenchurch Street to Barking C 20 8
Festiniog - 50 yrs of enterprise C 83 3
Festiniog 1946-55 E 01 7 - PUB 21 APRIL
Festiniog in the Fifties B 68 8
Festiniog in the Sixties B 91 6
Finsbury Park to Alexandra Palace C 02 4
Frome to Bristol B 77 0
Fulwell - Trams, Trolleys & Buses D 11 1
G
Gloucester to Bristol D 35 7
Gloucester to Cardiff D 66 1
Gosport & Horndean Trys B 92 3
Gosport - Branch Lines around A 36 9
Great Yarmouth Tramways D 13 5
Greece Narrow Gauge D 72 2
Greenwich & Dartford Tramways B 14 5 OOP
Grimsby & Cleethorpes Trolleybuses D 86 9
Guildford to Redhill A 63 5 OOP
H
Hammersmith & Hounslow Trys C 33 8
Hampshire Narrow Gauge D 36 4
Hampshire Waterways A 84 0 OOP
Hampstead & Highgate Tramways B 53 4
Harrow to Watford D 14 2
Hastings to Ashford A 37 6
Hastings Tramways B 18 3
Hastings Trolleybuses B 81 7 OOP
Hawkhurst - Branch Line to A 66 6
Hay-on-Wye - Branch Lines around D 92 0
Hayling - Branch Line to A 12 3
Haywards Heath to Seaford A 28 4
Hemel Hempstead - Branch Lines to D 88 3
Henley, Windsor & Marlow - BL to C77 2
Hereford to Newport D 54 8
Hexham to Carlisle D 75 3
Hitchin to Peterborough D 07 4
Holborn & Finsbury Tramways B 79 4
Holborn Viaduct to Lewisham A 81 9
Horsham - Branch Lines to A 02 4
Huddersfield Tramways D 95 1
Huddersfield Trolleybuses C 92 5
Hull Tramways D60 9
Hull Trolleybuses D 24 1
Huntingdon - Branch Lines around A 93 2
I
Ilford & Barking Tramways B 61 9
Ilford to Shenfield C 97 0
Ilfracombe - Branch Line to B 21 3
Ilkeston & Glossop Tramways D 40 1
Industrial Rlys of the South East A 09 3
Ipswich to Saxmundham C 41 3
Ipswich Trolleybuses D 59 3
Isle of Wight Lines - 50 yrs C 12 3
K
Keighley Tramways & Trolleybuses D 83 8
Kent & East Sussex Waterways A 72 X
Kent Narrow Gauge C 45 1
Kent Seaways - Hoys to Hovercraft D 79 1
Kidderminster to Shrewsbury E10 9
Kingsbridge - Branch Line to C 98 7
Kingston & Hounslow Loops A 83 3 OOP
Kingston & Wimbledon Tramways B 56 5
Kingswear - Branch Line to C 17 8
L
Lambourn - Branch Line to C 70 3
Launceston & Princetown - BL to C 19 2
Lewisham & Catford Tramways B 26 8 OOP
Lewisham to Dartford A 92 5
Lines around Wimbledon B 75 6
Liverpool Street to Chingford D 01 2
Liverpool Street to Ilford C 34 5
Liverpool Tramways - Eastern C 04 8
Liverpool Tramways - Northern C 46 8
Liverpool Tramways - Southern C 23 9
London Bridge to Addiscombe B 20 6
London Bridge to East Croydon A 58 1
London Chatham & Dover Railway A 88 8
London Termini - Past and Proposed D 00 5
London to Portsmouth Waterways B 43 5
Longmoor - Branch Lines to A 41 3
Looe - Branch Line to C 22 2
Lyme Regis - Branch Line to A 45 1
Lynton - Branch Line to B 04 6
M
Maidstone & Chatham Tramways B 40 4
Maidstone Trolleybuses C 00 0 OOP
March - Branch Lines around B 09 1
Margate & Ramsgate Tramways C 52 9
Marylebone to Rickmansworth D49 4
Melton Constable to Yarmouth Beach E 03 1
Midhurst - Branch Lines around A 49 9
Midhurst - Branch Lines to A 01 7 OOP
Military Defence of West Sussex A 23 9
Military Signals, South Coast C 54 3
Minehead - Branch Line to A 80 2
Mitcham Junction Lines B 01 5
Mitchell & company C 59 8
Monmouthshire Eastern Valleys D 71 5
Moreton-in-Marsh to Worcester D 26 5
Moretonhampstead - BL to C 27 7
Mountain Ash to Neath D 80 7
N
Newbury to Westbury C 66 6
Newcastle to Hexham D 69 2
Newcastle Trolleybuses D 78 4
Newport (IOW) - Branch Lines to A 26 0
Newquay - Branch Lines to C 71 0
Newton Abbot to Plymouth C 60 4
Northern France Narrow Gauge C 75 8
North East German Narrow Gauge D 44 9
North Kent Tramways B 44 2
North London Line B 94 7
North Woolwich - BLs around C 65 9
Norwich Tramways C 40 6
Nottinghamshire & Derbyshire T/B D 63 0
Nottinghamshire & Derbyshire T/W D 53 1
O
Ongar - Branch Lines to E 05 5
Orpington to Tonbridge B 03 9 OOP
Oxford to Bletchley D57 9
Oxford to Moreton-in-Marsh D 15 9
P
Paddington to Ealing C 37 6
Paddington to Princes Risborough C 81 9
Padstow - Branch Line to B 54 1
Plymouth - BLs around B 98 5
Plymouth to St. Austell C 63 5
Pontypool to Mountain Ash D 65 4
Porthmadog 1954-94 - BL around B 31 2
Porthmadog to Blaenau B 50 3 OOP
Portmadoc 1923-46 - BL around B 13 8
Portsmouths Tramways B 72 5
Portsmouth to Southampton A 31 4
Portsmouth Trolleybuses C 73 4
Potters Bar to Cambridge D 70 8
Princes Risborough - Branch Lines to D 05 0
Princes Risborough to Banbury C 85 7
R
Railways to Victory C 16 1 OOP
Reading to Basingstoke B 27 5
Reading to Didcot C 79 6
Reading to Guildford A 47 5 OOP
Reading Tramways B 87 9
Reading Trolleybuses C 05 5
Redhill to Ashford A 73 4
Return to Blaenau 1970-82 C 64 2
Rickmansworth to Aylesbury D 61 6
Roman Roads of Hampshire D 67 8
Roman Roads of Kent E 02 4
Roman Roads of Surrey C 61 1
Roman Roads of Sussex C 48 2
Romneyrail C 32 1
Ryde to Ventnor A 19 2
S
Salisbury to Westbury B 39 8
Salisbury to Yeovil B 06 0 OOP
Saxmundham to Yarmouth C 69 7
Saxony Narrow Gauge D 47 0
Seaton & Eastbourne Tramways B 76 3 OOP
Seaton & Sidmouth - Branch Lines to A 95 6
Secret Sussex Resistance B 82 4
SECR Centenary album C 11 6
Selsey - Branch Line to A 04 8
Sheerness - Branch Lines around B 16 9
Shepherds Bush to Uxbridge T/Ws C 28 4
Shrewsbury - Branch Line to A 86 4
Sierra Leone Narrow Gauge D 28 9
Sirhowy Valley Line E 12 3
Sittingbourne to Ramsgate A 90 1
Slough to Newbury C 56 7
Solent - Creeks, Crafts & Cargoes D 52 4
Southamptons Tramways B 33 6
Southampton to Bournemouth A 42 0
Southend-on-Sea Tramways B 28 2
Southern France Narrow Gauge C 47 5
Southwark & Deptford Tramways B 38 1
Southwold - Branch Line to A 15 4
South Eastern & Chatham Railways C 08 6
South London Line B 46 6
South London Tramways 1903-33 D 10 4
South London Tramways 1933-52 D 89 0
South Shields Trolleybuses E 11 6
St. Albans to Bedford D 08 1
St. Austell to Penzance C 67 3
St. Pancras to Barking D 68 5
St. Pancras to St. Albans C 78 9
Stamford Hill Tramways B 85 5
Steaming through Cornwall B 30 5 OOP
Steaming through Kent A 13 0 OOP
Steaming through the Isle of Wight A 56 7
Steaming through West Hants A 69 7
Stratford upon avon to Birmingham D 77 7
Stratford upon Avon to Cheltenham C 25 3
Strood to Paddock Wood B 12 1 OOP
Surrey Home Guard C 57 4
Surrey Narrow Gauge C 87 1
Surrey Waterways A 51 2 OOP
Sussex Home Guard C 24 6
Sussex Narrow Gauge C 68 0
Sussex Shipping Sail, Steam & Motor D 23 4 O
Swanley to Ashford B 45 9
Swindon to Bristol C 96 3
Swindon to Gloucester D46 3
Swindon to Newport D 30 2
Swiss Narrow Gauge C 94 9
T
Talyllyn - 50 years C 39 0
Taunton to Barnstaple B 60 2
Taunton to Exeter C 82 6
Tavistock to Plymouth B 88 6
Tees-side Trolleybuses D 58 6
Tenterden - Branch Line to A 21 5
Thanets Tramways B 11 4 OOP
Three Bridges to Brighton A 35 2
Tilbury Loop C 86 4
Tiverton - Branch Lines around C 62 8
Tivetshall to Beccles D 41 8
Tonbridge to Hastings A 44 4
Torrington - Branch Lines to B 37 4
Tunbridge Wells - Branch Lines to A 32 1
Twickenham & Kingston Trys C 35 2
Two-Foot Gauge Survivors C 21 5 OOP
U
Upwell - Branch Line to B 64 0
V
Victoria & Lambeth Tramways B 49 7
Victoria to Bromley South A 98 7
Victoria to East Croydon A 40 6 OOP
Vivarais C 31 4 OOP
Vivarais Revisited E 08 6
W
Walthamstow & Leyton Tramways B 65 7
Waltham Cross & Edmonton Trys C 07 9
Wandsworth & Battersea Tramways B 63 3
Wantage - Branch Line to D 25 8
Wareham to Swanage - 50 yrs D 09 8
War on the Line A 10 9
War on the Line VIDEO + 88 0
Waterloo to Windsor A 54 3
Waterloo to Woking A 38 3
Watford to Leighton Buzzard D 45 6
Wenford Bridge to Fowey C 09 3
Westbury to Bath B 55 8
Westbury to Taunton C 76 5
West Cornwall Mineral Railways D 48 7
West Croydon to Epsom B 08 4
West German Narrow Gauge D 93 7
West London - Branch Lines of C 50 5
West London Line B 84 8
West Sussex Waterways A 24 6 OOP
West Wiltshire - Branch Lines of D 12 8
Weymouth - Branch Lines around A 65 9
Willesden Junction to Richmond B 71 8
Wimbledon to Beckenham C 58 1
Wimbledon to Epsom B 62 6
Wimborne - Branch Lines around A 97 0
Wisbech - Branch Lines around C 01 7
Wisbech 1800-1901 C 93 2
Woking to Alton A 59 8
Woking to Portsmouth A 25 3
Woking to Southampton A 55 0
Wolverhampton Trolleybuses D 85 2
Woolwich & Dartford Trolleys B 66 4
Worcester to Birmingham D 97 5
Worcester to Hereford D 38 8
Worthing to Chichester A 06 2
Y
Yeovil - 50 yrs change C 38 3
Yeovil to Dorchester A 76 5 OOP
Yeovil to Exeter A 91 8
York Tramways & Trolleybuses D 82 1